SOCCER
COACHING

To my parents Malcolm and Charlotte for their love, sacrifices and encouragement throughout my football career and life. I was coached by the best and I still miss them.

Malcolm Cook was born in Scotland. As a youth he represented his country at amateur level, before turning pro with Motherwell. He went on to play for Bradford City and Newport County before a knee injury prematurely ended his playing career. After training as a teacher and rising to Head of Sport at a Yorkshire Grammar school, he returned to professional football as coach at Doncaster Rovers, Bradford City, Huddersfield Town and Liverpool, where he was appointed Director of Youth by Kenny Dalglish MBE. Malcolm once again went back to education, gaining degrees in Education Theory and Sports Psychology, and becoming a senior lecturer in Sports Studies. Now a UEFA/FA 'A' Licence coach, he is the author of five bestselling soccer books, including *Soccer Training, 101 Youth Soccer Drills (age 7 to 11)* and *101 Youth Soccer Drills (age 12 to 16)*, all published by A & C Black. Now residing in West Yorkshire, Malcolm is Executive Director of his own company, Freeflow Coaching, and is married with two daughters and three grandchildren.

SOCCER
COACHING
THE PROFESSIONAL WAY

A&
C B
& C BLACK • LONDON

MALCOLM COOK

Published in 2006 by
A & C Black Publishers Ltd
38 Soho Square, London W1D 3HB
www.acblack.com

ISBN-10: 0 7136 7485 7
ISBN-13: 978 0 7136 7485 9

A CIP record for this book is available from the
British Library.

Note: While every effort has been made to ensure
that the content of this book is as technically
accurate and as sound as possible, neither the
author nor the publisher can accept responsibility
for any injury or loss sustained as a result of the use
of this material.

A & C Black uses paper produced with elemental
chlorine-free pulp, harvested from managed
sustainable forests.

Acknowledgements
Cover illustration and design by James Watson
Inside illustrations by Mark Silver

Printed and bound in Great Britain by MPG Books
Limited

CONTENTS

ACKNOWLEDGEMENTS

I would like to thank the many soccer coaches who have influenced the way I think about the game; in particular, my brother-in-law Ricky Bow Sr, who was my first coach and guided me the correct way as a young player, and Allen Wade, the former Technical Director at the Football Association, who provided me with an excellent model of coaching in which to develop and grow.

Thanks also to another two talented coaches: Matt Driver, former coach to the New England Revolution, USA, for his continued support; and Darren Laver, Sport Evolution, for assisting me in typing the book.

Finally I am indebted to Andy Roxburgh and Allan Irvine, both of whom I hold in high regard, not only for their considerable coaching ability but also for their steadfast character. I thank them for their generous forewords.

FOREWORDS

Soccer history is full of the names of coaches and players who, like shooting stars in the night, lit up the game for a moment, only to disappear without trace. By contrast, there are many unsung stalwarts who have contributed to the quality of the game over a long period of time without seeking the spotlight. Malcolm Cook falls into the latter category.

For many decades as a pro, Malcolm has shone his light down the path of soccer development. Many have benefited from his guidance and recognised his passionate commitment to the game that we both fell in love with in our native town of Glasgow. Dark, damp streets were the breeding ground for bright football ideas and dreams of stardom played out under floodlit skies. Malcolm is from the very heart of the game, a pragmatic thinker and light years away from the sterile theorist.

I have detected a change of mentality in Britain to coach education and, like the progressive nations from Continental Europe and beyond, there is a growing realisation that the creative development of coaches and players is vital for any nation wishing to be successful at the top level of the game. *Soccer Coaching: the Professional Way* is a wonderful guide for those who see complacency as stagnation and fresh ideas as advancement. Through the pages of this book, Malcolm plays you – the coach – an outstanding pass. He has done the hard work and now it is up to you to produce the results. You can become the star in the limelight while he glows with contentment in the background, knowing that once again he has contributed to the advancement of soccer.

Andy Roxburgh
UEFA Technical Director
Former Scottish National Coach

As a coach, I am always looking at ways to enhance my own development. *Soccer Coaching: the Professional Way* is a comprehensive resource that will greatly assist me in becoming a better coach. The book covers all the essentials that are all-too-often missed in other manuals of its kind. It is full of excellent ideas, coaching tools, practical activities, explanations of key factors for the coach and much more. I find it a first-class coaching guide, which I will utilise for a long time to come.

Allan Irvine
Assistant Manager, Everton Football Club

INTRODUCTION

Soccer coaching in the modern game has become a complex occupation, involving the effective understanding and application of important principles, knowledge and skills. The coach must communicate well, make clear decisions whilst under pressure, and be able to handle players of various temperaments. He must possess great knowledge of the game with the capacity to plan, organise and execute a programme of quality practice sessions for his players. He also requires a keen tactical mind and the strength of character to cope with stress brought on by the ever-growing demand for instant success.

There are positive signs that, as a nation, we are at last beginning to appreciate the need for a more detailed, in-depth and professional approach to coaching if we are going to compete seriously in world soccer. I have spent decades of study compiling the contents for this book, which stem mainly from my own experiences as a player, coach and coach-educator. To further supplement my knowledge, I have drawn from information and research contained in selected technical manuals plus discussions with many top-class coaches and the analytical observation of many of them in action. There is little about tactics, technical skills or strategy in the book – there are numerous manuals on the market to supply this information and knowledge. This book is more about the nuts and bolts of the coaching process – the 'how to coach' rather than the 'what to coach'. My experiences have allowed me to reach some conclusions about this demanding occupation and although the book is entitled *Soccer Coaching: the Professional Way*, it does not mean it is purely aimed at the professional game. The word is used in terms of best practice, and any soccer coach, at whatever level of the game he works, can benefit from the contents and be just as professional in his approach.

The book does not attempt to provide definitive answers or solutions for all coaches; the problems vary too much for each individual who will have their own unique way of doing things. The aim is to set down the major areas of the soccer coaching process and suggest guidelines, which coaches can consider to achieve success. My hope is that this book will provide a positive reference source for the coach, which will allow him to develop players and teams that are a credit to himself and to the game.

Malcolm Cook

Note

Throughout the book coaches and players are referred to individually as he. This should be taken to mean he or she where appropriate.

CHAPTER 1
PLANNING THE COACHING PROGRAMME

To be consistently successful, the coach must prepare his team thoroughly over months and years of high-quality practice so they reach their maximum potential – there are no shortcuts!

It is easy to see over-anxious coaches who have failed to do this planning, charging about before and during the match, frantically trying to give their players last-minute instructions, which they cannot possibly take in. They are already mentally and emotionally charged-up for the match, so he will only succeed in transmitting his own worries to the already nervous players, which will, almost certainly, lower their performances.

The successful coach does not hope that everything will be ok on the day; he will not leave things to chance but will prepare his team thoroughly to meet the demands of the match. By sound planning and organisation, the coach will provide the team with a sense of direction, purpose and realism throughout the coaching programme. Without this, the practice sessions will fail to provide the players with clear objectives to aim for throughout the season.

The season is a marathon, not a sprint – for the coach a players alike, the season can seem a long time. It is traditionally broken into three short 'chunks', which interlink with each other. This allows for a more cohesive, progressive and natural way to plan and deliver the coaching programme. These phases are pre-season, competitive season and post-season.

PRE-SEASON PHASE

This is when the players return to training after a break from the last playing season. It is when they prepare for the start of the next phase, the competitive season. This phase is split into two smaller parts, which aim to slip smoothly into each other to avoid or lessen injuries, and to ensure maximum progression.

The first part is **general**. It concentrates on safe, basic, gradual work to build a solid foundation for the more intensive coaching work which will follow. The second part is when the start of the playing season approaches, and there is a transition towards more **specific work**. This will be aimed at building from the more general (e.g. technical skills, small group functional work, aerobic running, etc.) to the more specific (e.g. tactical rehearsal, patterns of play and systems, speed and agility running, etc.) The coach must not try to do too much, too soon in this phase. Try to start to develop a weekly training rhythm, which will continue throughout the season.

COMPETITIVE PHASE

Ideally, players should be fully integrated into this phase by the first competitive match of the season – the practice is over; it is performance time!

In reality, it will be very difficult to get each individual player, and the team as a whole, fully match-fit by this time. The coach will be trying for early results at this stage, where it is important to get off to a good start. However, he needs to be aware of pushing his players too much at the start and ending up with one or two key players injured – a delicate balance to achieve! This phase is the longest and most difficult one for the coach and players, who will be tested throughout its duration. The aim is to grow as individuals and as a team over the season plus to win matches – pure and simple! We are all affected by results, but the coach must get his players into a weekly routine with which they are comfortable *whatever* the score on match day.

This is where you as coach come into your own – you need to plan well, trust your programme and stick with it to make it work.

POST-SEASON PHASE

This is when the competitive phase of the season ends and the players have a period of rest from the rigours of the year. They need psychological, physical and emotional recovery away from the pressure of competition. This is the time to go on holiday, do different stimulating activities and to recharge their batteries. They should aim to recover some of the energy they have lost during the season, although they must avoid the extremes of over-eating, lack of sleep, inactivity or other negative lifestyle habits. Any advantages gained by relaxation can be off set by physical deterioration (e.g. becoming overweight, decreased strength and endurance, sluggish thinking, etc.), so there needs to be a balance between some active work to maintain mind/body fitness and good quality rest to allow full recovery from the stresses of the previous season. Coaches could, in agreement with their players, set goals or standard post-season programmes related to body-weight, nutrition and diet, fitness, mental-training or technical skills. This however needs to be done with the players' cooperation to have full effect.

PLANNING THE COACHING SESSION

The coach should plan and conduct his coaching sessions on sound principles, which enhance the learning process for all his players and the team. The following model provides a systematic approach to delivering effective sessions to assist the coach to achieve this.

The starting point is the planned season programme from which each session is derived. The coaching sessions prepare the team for the forth-coming competitive match, where their performances are evaluated. From this experience, adjustments may be made to the programme (shown by the jagged line on the diagram overleaf) before the system starts again.

Planning

This is often badly done by coaches who simply go through the motions, hoping players will learn from unstructured practice. Such practices have little relevance to the players' or team's needs, and do little to improve or prepare them for the actual match. The professional coach will take the time needed to think through and plan what he wants to do with his players. This process will ensure that he covers, and memorises, the essential information that he wishes to get across to them. The coaching session sheet on page 5 demonstrates how he might plan his session.

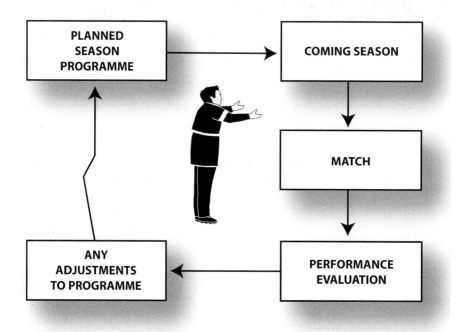

The sheet covers one week and has spaces for dates, week numbers, coaching goals, and a training and coaching load scale. The coach can plan the intensity of the weekly load at the weekend by filling in the appropriate column with a highlighter pen. In this way, he has a clear picture of the daily coaching load. To complete the plan, there are spaces where the coach can enter his daily practical contents, meetings, match(s) and a final summary. The sheet can then be photocopied for the season. He could also make some small cards with more practical details such as coaching areas, key coaching points, drills and activities, etc., which he can carry in his tracksuit pocket, referring to them when needed during the session.

Organising

Players, space, time and equipment need to be organised quickly and without fuss to gain maximum benefit from the practice. The players need to listen to all instructions and be in a position to see any demonstrations given by the coach. The coach must ensure that the group is positioned close together and that distractions such as the sun shining directly in their eyes, excessive noise coming

PRO WAY COACHING SESSION CHECKLIST

□ **WEEK NO.** **MONTH** _____ **DATE** _____ to _____

Goals for the week

Match								Technical
Heavy								
Moderate								Physical
Light								
Rest								Tactical
	M	T	W	T	F	S	S	

Mental

Days	**Session Contents**	**Notes/Meetings**
Monday		
Tuesday		
Wednesday		
Thursday		
Friday		
Saturday	Match v	
Week Summary		

from any source and the wind blowing directly towards him which can prevent his voice from being heard by the players, are avoided. He needs to demonstrate exactly what he wishes them to do and quickly arrange relevant practice in small groups.

Observing

While the players are practising, the coach needs to get into the best possible position to see what is happening. His position will change, as at times he will stand back to gain a greater over view of the practice whilst at other times he will get closer to the action so he can pinpoint exactly what aspects require working on. What the coach decides to observe will depend on his experience, knowledge of the game and coaching style. He needs to ensure he does not get in the way and obstruct the flow of the practice – instead he should move around to look at situations from various positions.

Communicating

The coach and players communicate, not only verbally, but also through their eyes, ears and bodies. It is vital that the coach develops the ability to communicate well with the players by learning how to recognise, understand and use these senses during practice sessions. Generally, players learn more from seeing than from hearing. Cut down the verbal explanations and use demonstrations on the field of play whenever possible.

The way a coach talks to his players and attempts to transmit his ideas is important in the communication process. The voice can be used effectively to convey different things to different players. For example, if you want to issue orders that need to be carried out quickly, do it firmly and loudly whilst if you wish to motivate the players, you should talk more quickly and more enthusiastically, or slow your speech down to calm more the excitable players. Avoid bad speaking habits such as putting a hand over your mouth, mumbling or using coaching 'jargon' that players may not understand – these are not conducive to good communication.

The coach must also be aware of how much information is given away by body language. If you do not believe in what you are saying or are not sure about your subject or do not like some of the players who you are speaking to, no matter how good your act in trying to cover-up, the chances are your body will somehow communicate these feelings to the players in some way. The coach can learn to look for signs such as avoiding eye contact, defensive-stances with arms tightly crossed or standing very near or far away or other forms of behaviour, which could indicate blocks to good communication.

Reviewing

If there was one thing I learned during my spell as coach at Liverpool Football Club, it was the way that the coaches from the famous boot room reviewed each practice session straight afterwards. Whatever the weather, they wrote up their experiences in the legendary training diaries, noting what had happened during the session. The coach must evaluate each session, deciding what went well and what could have been done differently. This is his starting point for the next session and should include areas such as equipment, practice themes, the attitude of the players, methods and practices used, the effect of weather, etc. In this way, he can detect weaknesses and so avoid problems and design better practice sessions.

THE COACHING CYCLE

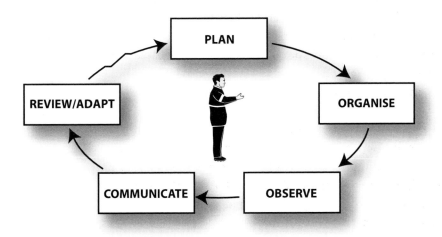

The coach needs to follow a systematic cycle of work where he plans his pro-gramme for the season and follows a set pattern where he can monitor and evaluate each week's training and coaching sessions, competitive matches and other relevant situations or events. The feedback provides material for the following week's coaching schedule.

Coaching format

To ensure progression, the coach should develop a coaching format which guarantees a structure for realistic work, which will transfer into the actual competitive game. The following format is one that I have used for many years and found to be productive. Other coaches may have a different, but equally successful format, it all depends on what you are comfortable with and what actually works!

Coaching system of work

Stage 1 – The whole game-like situation – demonstration

Organise a full 11 v 11 or some kind of smaller game situation and play for five to ten minutes. The coach allows players to see the 'big-picture' before selecting some aspect of the game to work on. Say, for example, he wishes to focus on getting both his wingbacks to get forward up the flanks more effectively. He could use the 'freeze' method of coaching to isolate a few situations where the wingbacks could push forward to support attacks (see page 34).

Stage 2 – Part coaching – repetition

The coach could set up dual practice on both sides of the field where the wingbacks work on timing their runs onto the ball and practice crossing techniques on the run. The opposition is largely unopposed at this stage so that the players can gain early success and get a simple picture of what is required.

Stage 3 – Part-whole progression – complex

Increase the complexity of the practice by introducing gradual opposition, less space, faster practice tempo, harder technical skills. The situation is more geared to the actual match situation and increases the decision-making and complexity for the wingbacks.

Stage 4 – Whole game situation – competitive

Organise a full 11 v 11 game or smaller, depending on the topic. The idea is to integrate the wingbacks into the new elements introduced. The coach can introduce conditioned play, which allows many opportunities for the wingbacks to push forward up the flanks and try to play crosses into the penalty box. The game can be left un-coached and played in a competitive manner so they can learn to apply newly-learned skills and knowledge in realistic conditions.

It is not always necessary to work from stage 1 up to stage 4 in each session – this is unrealistic because of the speed of things, the difficulty of the topic being introduced to the players, their level of ability and the practice time available plus other factors will affect practice. The coach must decide on the rate of progress – going too quickly is as bad as going too slowly. At times some of the stages can be omitted, when the players are ready for this.

The effect of fatigue

The coach must be aware of the effect of fatigue on his players' performance during a practice session. Fatigue affects the mind's ability to think clearly and to make good decisions, thus making reading of the game difficult. It also affects muscular rhythm, timing and coordination making skill performance hard to replicate. When learning and understanding new skills, the player should be fairly fresh in mind and body so he can receive, absorb and memorise information gained from the practice session. With this in mind, ensure that most intensive fitness sessions **follow**, not precede, the technical skills work. All this must be catered for when planning the programme.

Summary

The coach needs to pay attention to detail when planning his coaching programme. The following practice session checklist will help him to achieve this so that he can maximise all the team's resources over the season.

PRACTICE SESSION
CHECKLIST

PRE-SESSION PHASE 1 – PLANNING

- Plan your practice topic(s) based upon the **previous** match or practice session.
- Always **write down** your session-plan ... ink it – don't think it.

PRE-SESSION PHASE 2 – ORGANISATION

- Arrive at least 30 minutes before the scheduled practice session time to set up the area and equipment.
- Ensure water, medical kit and all equipment are available.
- Have some activities set up for the early arrivals.
- Start the practice on time.

DURING SESSION PHASE 3 – PREPARATION

- Talk briefly at the start – let players know the session outline.
- Explain the benefits of learning the topic(s) to the group.
- Get the group to set a few simple session goals.
- Ensure warm-up is related to the practice topic(s).
- Use lead-in activities to prepare players for main topic(s).

DURING SESSION PHASE 4 – COMMUNICATION

- Use demonstrations appropriately.
- Do not over talk. Use clear, simple and relevant language.
- Keep it simple – **stick to the key factors**.
- Use **positive** language, reinforcement and praise with all your players.
- Use the freeze method at start, but no more than three times during the whole session.
- Do not tell them everything – use **questions** so the group can find it out for themselves.

DURING SESSION PHASE 5 – LEARNING

- Ensure a supply of balls is always available.
- Use appropriate third of the field or area for realism.
- Use appropriate number of players to fit the space for effective transfer of training.
- Remember the whole-part-whole sequence for practice and learning effect.
- Use available coaches effectively.

DURING SESSION PHASE 6 – MOTIVATIONAL

- Keep all players **actively** involved in the practice.
- As coach, stay **enthusiastic** and **positive** throughout the practice session.
- Always finish with an un-coached game – no interruptions.

POST-SESSION PHASE 7 – REFLECTIVE

- Allow players time to cool-down, unwind, stretch and recover after the end of practice.
- Ask players questions related to practice to reinforce memory, understanding and learning.
- Give out information about future matches, practice or term details.
- Inform players how they have done after the session – **be positive**.
- Review the practice session with other coaches.
- End the session on time.

CHAPTER 2
THE LEARNING
PROCESS

To be effective the coach must understand the processes by which players learn to play soccer, since by knowing what is happening in the player's mental and physical make-up, he can accelerate their development. If he does not know what should happen psychologically, he will have to rely on methods of trial and error, which can prove to be chaotic and ineffective.

PRINCIPLES OF SKILL LEARNING

Motivation

The player must want to learn before he can improve. Some players have a burning desire to learn while others are not so keen and need stimulating and pushing to reach their maximum potential. The coach must design his practice sessions so that players are interested in what they are doing and experience continued success during the practice. These sessions should be varied as there is nothing more boring than doing the same thing day after day. Sometimes players (particularly young ones) play the fool because of a lack of variety and challenge in the practice sessions. It is best, however, if players are internally motivated, and the coach needs to encourage this.

Transfer of training

To have maximum impact, the practice set up by the coach must simulate the competitive game as much as possible. This requires close observation of the tactical situations, skills, techniques, physical movements, workload and mental stresses of the game. Players must practise in the conditions they will encounter in a match; for example, on varied pitches that might be hard, muddy, icy, of irregular surface or small in size. They must experience playing the game and maintaining their concentration when cold, fatigued, in rain and snow, or playing under floodlights. He must ensure that players play in the correct footwear, and with the correct size and weight of ball wherever possible. Many coaches, concerned about the possibility of their players being injured in practice, often prohibit normal tackling or slow down the speed of practice to reduce the risk of injury. By doing this they prevent their team from preparing realistically for what will confront them in a competitive match. After players have learned the basic skills and tactics of the game, increased pressure should be put on them gradually until they can produce these skills at match speed. During practice, the coach must always encourage players to play at full match speed as much as possible and also to challenge for the ball as they would in the actual game.

He must always have transfer of training in mind when preparing a coaching session making it as realistic as possible. Try to include an 11 v 11 practice match each week to ensure that what you do in training has the best opportunity to benefit the players in the actual match.

Players' participation

The coach will increase the players' understanding of the game if he involves them personally in what he is attempting to do. They will be motivated if they are involved and told what and why they are practising and what the coach is trying to achieve. In this way, he will make the players see the relationship between the practice situation and the competitive game, thus aiding the transfer of training. He must always encourage his players to question and discuss things with him and, equally, he must listen to what they have to say. Often players have positive suggestions to make which will benefit the player and the team. The more they participate in the practice sessions, the more likely they are to memorise ideas and use them in the actual match.

Quality practice

Soccer techniques, skills and tactics are best learned and developed through repeated practice. The length of a practice session will depend on the interest or mood of the players, the weather, the time of day and the degree of fatigue. All these factors can influence the effectiveness of practice. Often coaches pack too much into a session and end up confusing players who cannot take in all the information and therefore lose interest. A good maxim for the coach is 'the quality of practice is more important than the quantity'. It is better to do a little well, than a lot badly.

The best response from players is obtained by shorter periods of intensive work involving maximum mental concentration and game-like physical effort, followed by short recovery intervals with a change to lighter and more entertaining activities with the ball. For example, a practice session spent mainly on improving the system of play allows little time to improve individual techniques and skills, while a session spent on basic skills with individuals will do nothing to help group or team understanding. Coaches often cannot agree on whether it is best to work from the whole-part-whole or from the part-to-the-whole situation, the whole being the game and the part being a smaller part of the game. It depends on the coach, the players he has at his disposal and the practice environment, as sometimes players cannot see the relationship between the part situation and the game situation and thus the practice is ineffective. Often, from the players' point of view, it is better to start from the beginning, i.e. with a full game (this could be the last match that the team has played), and isolate this from the skills or tactical theme that the coach wants to practice with the players so they can all see clearly what and why they are practising.

Repetitive practice

Often coaches make the mistake of thinking that because some aspect of play performed during practice or during a match was successful, this will always be the case. This simply is not true: individual and team performances will fluctuate, and players tend to forget things that brought them success earlier unless they are constantly reminded. They must remember that players are individuals; some have better memories than others and retain information easily, whereas some will need more revision of lessons learned. By continually going over important aspects of play, players will understand and memorise situations from the practice session and try to apply them in the competitive match. He can also aid players' understanding and ability by constantly reminding them to ignore irrelevant details which will do nothing to improve their play. He should focus their attention on the things that really matter and emphasise them by repeated discussion and demonstration.

Players need to be constantly reminded about various aspects of play before they can be integrated into their playing system. But although repetition is important in coaching, it can restrict players' thinking and performance if practised on too narrow a theme, for example, through phase-play where the back four unit of the team is constantly conditioned to deliver long passes up to two central strikers without much variation.

Individual treatment

The coach is making a serious mistake if he treats all his players in the same fashion: they have different temperaments, habits and needs, and must be dealt with on that basis. Some will grasp ideas more quickly than others, while some methods and approaches will work better with one player than with another. The interaction between the coach and the player is very important. The state of mind of player and team will ebb and flow depending on the circumstances at the time, and players will react better when they are winning. This is the time when the coach can safely give the players more work, since they will be in the right frame of mind to practise and work harder. Players who are part of a team which is on a losing run must be treated more delicately, as they will be much more difficult to motivate because of loss of confidence, depression, staleness and, perhaps, frustration and anger. The following guidelines will help the coach put these principles into practice.

GUIDELINES FOR THE COACH

The desire to learn

The coach must convince the players that they need to improve some aspect of play and also to persuade them to accept his methods of achieving this. He must use his personality to sell the ideas to his players so that they can see that they will benefit from the new skill or tactic. For example, if a player is a good attacker but neglects his defensive role, he must convince him that both he and the team will benefit from a change of role. To do this, the coach must make the player see what it will do for him – perhaps in gaining him more esteem from his team-mates, or gaining praise and support from the coach, or having more of the ball to do the things he enjoys, such as dribbling at defenders.

Practice tempo

As practice progresses and the players' abilities and understanding improve, the coach must gradually introduce methods that duplicate competitive match situations. Early practices should be relatively free of pressure, either from the coach's interference or from the difficulty of the task. He should increase the intensity and speed of the practice, depending on the rate of progress of the players, and he can do this by involving the players in competition against themselves or other team-mates, or by setting them targets.

Evaluate progress

The coach must be able to measure the improvement or decline of individual and team performance over a period of time, so that he can assess the impact of his work. He can assess his team or individuals in a variety of ways – match analysis, evidence of goals for and against, etc. However, the ultimate test of the training programme must always be the competitive match, whether assessing individuals or the team. If what the coach has worked on with a player or with the team during the weeks of practice turns out to be right on match day then the practice has been a success and the player or team has gained maximum transfer. The coach needs to set effective goals for his players which will motivate them to practise and improve certain aspects of their performance.

The need for patience

Both coach and players will need to show patience when learning a new aspect of play. The coach must make players understand that there may be quick success when learning a new skill which will be followed by a period when, no matter what the player does, nothing seems to improve. Some coaches often panic and change their methods of approach too soon during this period. Instead, they must have the courage and patience to give their players and the new aspect of play the necessary time to improve: if the idea is sound and the coaching method is correct, it is just a matter of time before the player improves. Sometimes the coach must be prepared to see the performance of a player, or even the team, suffer in the short term, but in the confidence that they will improve in the long term. Individuals vary in their rate of learning – some forget things more quickly than others, some lack determination and lose heart easily, while some are prepared to work for a long time in the belief that they will improve. In such circumstances, players must be reassured by the coach that provided they are patient and persistent, success will definitely follow. However, this does require nerve from both the coach and the player.

DISTRACTIONS TO LEARNING

To be effective, the coach must be aware of, and try to get rid of, as many distractions as he can for himself and the players in order to achieve something of value from the practice sessions. The following factors will all affect practice sessions from time to time.

Fatigue

This affects the capacity of the players to make the necessary movements, to perform the technical skills, to concentrate and to make the correct decisions. Being alert is particularly important when introducing new skills or tactics. The technical and tactical work should normally be done when the players are relatively fresh so they can mentally absorb the information. Remember, fatigue is both physical and mental and one effects the other.

Noise

Noise can be a problem during training sessions because the coach will not be able to communicate if he cannot be heard. On the other hand, he can shout too much, as can other players involved in the practice. Players who are learning new skills or tactics, particularly younger ones, are often intimidated and confused by too much noise and consequently their performance suffers. Music which relays a rhythm can be an aid to practice, but watch the noise levels! Coaches should never shout or give verbal information when players already have enough on their minds trying to absorb the complex skills of the game without also trying to process words coming at them from the coach.

Over-coaching

In the early stages of learning, it is usually necessary for the coach to be heavily involved with the players, providing considerable verbal and visual guidance. However, as soon as the players show signs of understanding and progress, the coach's involvement can be reduced gradually. He can make too many decisions for the players so that they become too dependent on him. Players must not be so rigidly controlled that they cannot think for themselves, because during a competitive match they cannot rely on the coach. The players need time to practise alone using trial and error to fully assimilate the new technique.

Atmosphere

The weather and climatic conditions – wet or dry, windy or humid – will affect the mood of the players. The time of day, the training pitch or surrounding area, and the general mood of the team will also affect the training atmosphere. Often coaches try to battle on with a theme when it is apparent that the players are not receptive. It may be that he has not been able to create the correct atmosphere by his manner and methods, or it may be that the players are in a particular mood and he has failed to see that this needs attending to before any coaching can take place.

Lack of motivation

The players must want to learn and succeed before they start to improve. If the players come to the session apathetic, the coach must find ways to arouse and motivate them so that they want to get involved in the practice session. He can use whatever methods he thinks best; however, the use of suitable incentives and rewards, competition and attractive practice work – say, with the ball – are usually effective to this end.

Players' fears

It has been mentioned earlier that the coach can inhibit players, particularly younger ones, but the same also applies to older, more experienced players who can stifle the education of younger players by intimidating them to the point where they are afraid of trying new things. Older players sometimes exploit youngsters for their own benefit when they should be encouraging them to be creative and opening up options for them. Organising groups comprising the right blend of older and younger players can help to eliminate such difficulties. All players have hidden fears, self-doubts and insecurities about their day-to-day performance; a sensitive coach who takes players with him by gaining their respect can help to remove these negative factors through time.

TECHNIQUE AND SKILL

The difference between technique and skill, and how they are developed, has caused some confusion among soccer coaches over the years. Let us first try to define what they are and how they differ.

Technique

This is the ability to execute a solitary action in isolation from the game – for example, a type of pass, shot, a side-step or dummy, or a catch. The player can develop his individual techniques by practising against a rebound surface on his own. The mental decisions involved are minimal and are concerned only with how to perform the action of heading or passing without the distractions of other players.

Skill

This is the ability to be in the correct place at the correct time and to be able to select and use the correct technique on demand. Unlike technique, skill involves the player in making decisions relating to opponents and team-mates during the game, so the environment is more unpredictable.

Some players have a wider range of techniques and can make the ball 'talk', displaying excellent control and touch; despite this, however, they cannot use these techniques in the 'moving' game and therefore cannot be deemed to be skilful soccer players. Technique, therefore, is only a part of skill. The player has to be able to apply technique and skill in the heat of a competitive match where physical challenges from opponents afford little space or time for decisions and where the situation is constantly changing.

What does this knowledge mean for the coach? Here are some guidelines to consider.

1. In my opinion, players should be given the opportunity to practise techniques at some time without the hindrance of opposition. Youngsters practising a new technique can gain early success and confidence in this way.

2. As soon as improvement is shown in a player's performance, increased stress must be put on the execution of techniques. This can be applied in a variety of ways, e.g. by quickening the pace, by increasing the number of repetitions, by giving the player less space thereby demanding more accuracy, or by technical competitions.

3. The amount of time and the level the coach works at will depend on two main factors: whether he is working with a learner to develop the new technique, or whether he is working with good technical players and the objective is to maintain existing techniques.

4. Players must be encouraged to display a wide range of techniques by good demonstrations and practice at a fairly high tempo.

5. When the players are fairly technically competent they should be put in a situation involving co-operation with team-mates against opponents so that they have the opportunity to learn the decision-making skills necessary to exploit their techniques. It is important that all players are allowed to experiment to some extent with their choice of decisions, thus learning for themselves what is and is not possible.

6. When assessing a player's performance, it should be established by the coach whether faults are of a technical (physical action) or of a skilful (decision making) nature with the appropriate practice set-up to rectify the total skill.

7. The coach must set the level of practice for the players. He should allow plenty of time to practise, experiment and gain the confidence needed to reach the required standard of performance.

8. He should often finish the practice session with a conditioned game to test the newly-acquired techniques and skills in a smaller game. Finally, it is always a good idea to end with a coached and uncoached 11 v 11 game where ever possible in order to obtain maximum practice transfer.

SOCCER SKILL

Soccer is a game in which the players' contribution is concerned with on-the-ball and off-the-ball play, and the making of decisions in an ever-changing environment. A considerable amount of research has been done into what happens during an actual game in terms of play, and the following facts have emerged. (See the diagrams at the bottom of this page.)

In a 90-minute match, the ball will, on average, be 'dead' and out of play for 30 minutes due to re-starts and stoppages of one kind or another. In the 60 minutes of time remaining in an evenly-balanced match, both teams will have possession of the ball for approximately 30 minutes. Each player in the team will have possession of the ball for a longer or shorter duration, depending on their position in the team and their involvement in the game; however, each player on average will not have the ball for longer than one minute.

This means that the player, whether goalkeeper, defender, midfield player or striker, will be moving about the field for approximately 58 minutes without the ball. Approximately half of that time will be spent defending and the other half attacking for his team. Whatever his function during that time, he will constantly be making decisions and judgments about how he can best help his team – e.g. 'How close should I get to mark this man?', 'Should I cover a dangerous space or a man in this situation?', 'Can I draw a player out of position to allow my team-mate space?' or 'Can I get away from my marker to receive the ball from a team-mate?'.

It is easier to spot and appreciate what a player does on the ball, but more difficult to recognise good off-the-ball play. Both are important in developing skilful soccer.

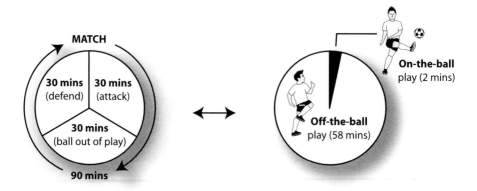

ANALYSING SKILL

As has been mentioned, for the larger part of the game the player does not have possession of the ball; therefore he spends his time making decisions about how best to help the attack or defence. When he has the ball he decides what to do to attack correctly. So whether he has the ball or not, there are three stages for the player and coach to analyse when deciding when skill breaks down.

1. **What** option to select from the alternatives available?

   Did the player select a reasonable option? Was a pass 'on' or should he have held on to the ball? Did he pass to the wrong player? Did he allow himself to be drawn out of position to mark an opponent, leaving a dangerous space for the opposition to exploit?

2. **How** will I do it?

   When the player has decided what option is best, he then decides how he is going to achieve his first objective.

3. **When** to execute the technique.

   After deciding how to do it, the player needs to execute the correct technique at the correct time for the situation. Here are some examples.

ATTACK

On the ball	Off the ball
A wing back running with the ball on the flank:	A striker awaits a throw-in being taken by one of his team-mates:
1 **What?** Decides to cross the ball into the penalty area.	1 **What?** Decides to decoy a certain defender away from an area of the field.
2 **How?** Decides to hit an out-swinging cross away from the goalkeeper to the far post area.	2 **How?** Decides to call for the ball and make a checkout movement.
3 **When?** Performs the technique before goalkeeper is correctly positioned.	3 **When?** Executes the run and takes the defender with him.

DEFENCE	
Off the ball	**On the ball**
Centre back sees play approach in front of him:	Goalkeeper catches a cross ball:
1 **What?** Decides to cover team-mate.	1 **What?** Decides to play the ball to a team-mate.
2 **How?** Considers his angle, distance and position.	2 **How?** Decides on an over arm throw. Execute his action quickly. Whether to punch or catch.
3 **When?** Leaves his opponent to get into the covering position.	3 **When?** Executes his action quickly to throw ball.

Skill can break down at any of the three levels and it is important that the coach realises that the player needs help in making the correct decisions, whether of a technical or a skilful nature, and this can only be done if the coach understands and identifies what is going wrong. Technique and skill are interdependent to a large extent. For example, time after time a player may fail to give a 25–35 m (30–40 yd) pass to an unmarked team-mate on the other side of the field. One reason may be that the player on the ball did not have the ability to get his head up and detect the team-mate, even though he might be an excellent all-round passer. The second reason could be that the player could certainly see the unmarked team-mate, but elected not to play the pass (which could have led to a goal for his team) because he did not have the confidence to execute the necessary technique with accuracy, so instead he played a shorter and more negative pass. The coach can see from these examples how limitations in technique can restrict players' skill.

Past experience

The player uses his past experiences to help him make decisions in a competitive game. For example, a striker is about to receive the ball with his back towards an opponent and has to make a quick decision on whether he should pass the ball first time, hold and screen the ball, or turn with the ball. He will tend to base his decisions on how successful he has been in the past in his response to this situation – 'feedback'. He may have tried to turn with the ball a few times before and found that he did not have the necessary control, speed or timing to elude his marker – so he cuts out that option. Often younger players make more elementary mistakes because, unlike older players, they do not have the number and variation of soccer experiences to draw upon. This is where the coach is vital. He can organise continuous practice where the player can gather the necessary experience to develop his game – although there is no better experience than in the match itself.

THE PHYSICAL AND MENTAL CONNECTION IN LEARNING

Each time a soccer player displays his skills or responds to situations, certain neuromuscular processes take place which the coach must understand.

The player sees a situation and decides to react. The mind sends messages to the muscles telling them they must act. The nerves are like telephone wires along which impulses pass to the various muscles of the body, and the speed at which the these messages pass along differs from player to player. When the message arrives at the muscles, two things can affect the reaction. Firstly, the state of preparation of the muscle (the muscle tone) is important. The muscle should be ready to spring into action, which can be done by a good warm-up and the correct mental concentration.

Secondly, the muscle should be as well developed and powerful as possible. Some players are very strong but are slow in movement and lack power relative to their bodyweight, while others may not have great strength but can use what they have with more speed and they are therefore more powerful.

The brain

The claim that soccer players have brains in their feet may sound convincing, but like many clichés it does not give an accurate or realistic account of the role the brain plays in the game of soccer. For example, a striker breaks clear of the defence with the ball at his feet in a race towards goal. The sort of information coming in to the player could be: 'Should I go all the way on my own or look for a team-mate approaching?', 'Have I the speed and strength to beat the recovering defenders?' or 'How near are they to me?'. The player will see the goal getting nearer and may see the anxiety on the goalkeeper's face for a fleeting moment; he will hear the crowd shout and will feel his nerves tighten. He may notice a muddy area on the edge of the penalty area and decide that he should take avoiding action. Through good training the striker may store some of this information in his memory-bank for future reference. Other pieces of information may be discarded by the brain as being irrelevant to the situation, e.g. an opponent who can be seen out of the corner of the player's eye but is too far away to disturb him. The brain can be likened to human computer, which gathers information, processes it, decides on actions to take and then sends the body into action. Coaches need to understand the vital importance the brain plays in the performance of the game of soccer – the ones who take the time and effort to do this will be richly rewarded.

The nervous system

Movement is caused by electrical impulses transmitted by the brain to the muscles via the nerves. Each message 'burns' a passageway, which makes it a little easier to repeat the message, movement and skill next time. Many thousands of repetitions develop a so-called 'groove' or habit – it's just as easy to develop bad habits as good ones and very difficult to eradicate bad habits which have been well grooved. It is important, therefore, that the coach sees that players practise correctly at all times, so that eventually players can trust their brains and bodies to repeat the technical skills and responses of the game automatically, freeing their minds to think about more immediate factors, such as the tactical reading of the game, analysing opponents, and the state of play. Less-skilled players always seem to be fighting for control of the ball and have to do things in a hurry. Skilful players, on the other hand, often have better physical 'touch' and control, and greater anticipation; therefore they have more time available and the freedom to execute their skills accurately.

Habits – good and bad

Many people in soccer talk about players developing good habits. What do they mean by this? Many of the players' technical skills, movements and responses can be quickened and conditioned so that they are performed almost without thinking. There are dangers in this sort of learning, however, for if a coach ingrains into a player the wrong response to a situation, it is difficult for the player to get out of the habit. For example, a player may play the shortest and easiest pass that he sees each time he has the ball, when it is obvious that more effective passes are open to him; or a full back, seeing that his winger has the ball, suddenly bursts forwards on an overlap run down the flank time after time, using up precious energy and gaining no advantage for his team. Both these responses may be the product of bad coaching.

The soccer player needs to be able to make speedy decisions after examining the situation building up around him. For example, a midfield player in possession of the ball in the attacking third of the field may have to decide whether to pass the ball, hold on to it and wait for more support, or go it alone and try to shoot at goal. He has only fractions of a second in which to make his decision, otherwise he will lose possession of the ball and the attacking opportunity of his team. A player can be trained to make speedier and more accurate decisions incisively by cutting out bad habits, such as selfish play, conceding free kicks or penalties, bad tackling or being caught in possession. The coach must attempt to replace bad habits with good ones. All this needs is patience and sensitivity.

PERFORMANCE MODEL

The simplified model below of the physical and mental processes involved in human performance gives an idea of the functioning of the player's system. The system basically works like this: the player sees a situation and information from what he sees is relayed via the senses (eyes, ears, muscles, etc.) to the central mechanism of the brain. Here it is processed and decisions are made on what needs to be done in a particular situation. Finally, the appropriate muscular response is made and the player performs the movement in order to execute the technical skill or tactical action required. Feedback can be used by the player immediately or can be stored in his memory for future use. The coach is very important to the player's knowledge of how he has performed, for example, in the technical execution of striking the ball or in his tactical response to a situation where he was defending with two attackers approaching him and his goal with the ball at speed. The player can make errors either by selecting the wrong information from the situation, or by interpreting the information from the sense incorrectly, or by timing the muscular movements incorrectly.

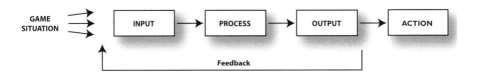

Demonstration

Coaches need to get ideas across to players quickly. The ability of the coach to set up meaningful demonstrations is a most important part of his job and he should note the following factors.

Clear picture

The old maxim that one picture is worth a thousand words is often true, and very much so in soccer coaching. The visual demonstration gives a quick and clear picture which can be repeated over and over again. The coach should go through demonstrations at different speeds for the sake of clarity. Instant video systems which show players or teams in action are excellent for providing feedback.

Motivation

If the demonstration is a good one, it will often have a motivational effect on the players who will wish to practise so that they can repeat and learn the skill for themselves. It is important therefore that the demonstrational model is a realistic and effective one and good performers should be selected for this reason.

Key factors

The coach should help the players to identify key factors in the performance of a skill by the use of verbal instructions given in a brief and effective way. At the first demonstration, it will be difficult to focus players' attention on technical points as they will tend to look at the skill aesthetically as a whole. But gradually they will accept technical information about the skill. The coach should focus his players on key factors such as leg position, body rotation to kick, etc., as they observe the skill in action.

Exactness

The demonstration is a model for the players or team to copy until an acceptable level of competence and performance is achieved. The coach must allow players to develop their own natural responses, comply with principles which suit their physical and mental make-up and not merely mimic the demonstration. The idea is to get a good visual image of the skill which can be referred to by the players for development.

Summary

The coach must understand the physical and psychological principles by which players learn to play soccer because errors in his handling can greatly retard a player's ultimate progress and development. He needs to set up effective practices which stimulate and challenge his players and help them to solve their own problems on the field rather than depending on him to find the answers.

CHAPTER 3
COACHING METHODS

THE TOOLS OF THE TRADE

To gain the maximum benefit from each practice session, the coach must select the most productive method for the particular coaching situation. He must also build on his experience of using them so that he can adapt the methods to fit the everyday circumstances that he and his players will encounter. For example, on a cold, wet and miserable day it would not be desirable to use a method which necessitates having to stop practice play frequently. The players would have to stand idly by, listening to the coach's instructions whilst feeling chilled, damp and frustrated – hardly an ideal learning environment! Similarly, it would be unwise to work on developing individual ball techniques with a large group of players when there are only one or two footballs. Many players will be inactive for longish periods of the practice session, missing the repetition of making contact with the ball – this is not conducive to motivation or effective learning.

The coach must give serious thought to the methods he will employ when planning his session and the probable effect it will have on his players' overall on-going development. Remember, although as coaches we all have our favourite method, no one way is best for all circumstances. We must learn to widen our scope to the point where we eventually feel comfortable using a variety of ways to reach, motivate and develop our players.

When considering which method to use during your coaching session, think carefully about these key factors before you decide.

1. **Objective**

   What is the intention of the practice session and what do you hope to achieve? Is it designed for individuals, a group or the whole squad of players? Do you want to work on individual technique, group skill, physical conditioning, team tactics and teamwork or developing the systems of play? Is the session more geared to building mental qualities? What is the general theme of the practice session? Some methods will suit a theme more than others, so be clear about the session objective when selecting your methods.

2. **Attitude**

   What is the team's general mood and attitude to practice at the moment? Are they, on the whole, positive or negative? Are they on a winning or losing run of matches at this time? It is almost always easier to do your coaching when the team is having success of the field – most methods seem to work in these circumstances! The challenge for the coach is when the players' spirits are down and they need a psychological lift.

   Certain methods, such as high-tempo drills or small-sided games can be used for shortish periods with good effect to shake players out of their lethargy. There is no better feeling for a coach than starting a practice session with a group of dispirited players and ending up with them buzzing with activity! Motivating players who are reluctant to practice correctly is a challenge for all coaches. They must be responsible for their players' attitude to practice – selecting and using the correct methods is the coach's way of aiding this process in a positive way.

3. **Weather**

   What is the general climate and atmosphere like – is it cold, humid, grey, windy, wet, etc? The weather can have a massive effect on the quality of your practice session. As coach, you cannot control the weather but you can do something about the general atmosphere as it affects your session. The first thing to be aware of is how we (yourself included) can be influenced by the weather so, as coaches, we need to take a lead and ensure that we do not convey any depressive signs to the players, even though we may be frustrated at another day of rain which forces us to cancel our coaching plans again! Obviously, players need to learn to be adaptable to the various climatic conditions they play in. However, the coach can use methods on the more 'extreme' days which can stimulate them to the point where they begin to forget their discomfort and become absorbed in the practice work.

4. Facilities and Equipment

What practice fields and areas (indoor or outdoor) are available? What condition are they in – flat, bumpy, grass or artificial turf? If the weather changes, can you work indoors? The quality of your coaching facilities can have a big effect on the methods you choose as coach. Most of us have had to improvise because of a lack of facilities during our coaching careers and have used dressing rooms, car parks, etc. – coaches do not always need expensive facilities or equipment, however, good ones will have an effect on the chosen coaching method.

The coach should check how many footballs, training bibs, portable goals, marker cones and other coaching aids he has at his disposal. Good equipment can provide a more attractive and challenging practice environment with more options for the players. The quality of your facilities and equipment will have a considerable bearing on the selection of your coaching methods.

5. Players

How many players are available for practice? Who are they? What standard, experience and positions do they play? Are key players missing? This may mean you need to change the tactical options which you had intended to work with. For example, what happens if you intend to set up a realistic shooting practice for your strikers but find that you have no goalkeeper available? The number of players that you have during a practice session will force you, as coach, to think about the best methods to use in these circumstances.

6. Coaches

Do you continually work with the group on your own or are other fellow coaches available to assist? Some coaches take 'ownership' of their squad and no-one else is allowed access to them in practice. This is an unfortunate view to adopt, as, by co-operating with other coaches, the group could be split into smaller, more manageable units, which could allow you to work more closely with some of your players and improve the quality of the practice. By using and organising the coaches more carefully, it will give you the opportunity to use more methods which are appropriate to the players at various times.

COACHING METHOD BREAKDOWN

The following section will give you a description of some of the most-used coaching methods in the modern game. Coaches are resourceful and, through practice, experience and experimentation, will start to form their own coaching styles. Quite naturally they will begin to refine the way they use the methods, making them their own through time.

We have shown clear examples of each coaching method, plus a detailed breakdown with explanations, analysis and suggestions for the coach – in this way they can get the best from the players.

Method 1 – Freeze-play

This method is one in which the coach signals for the players to stop instantly, whilst they are in the playing. He does this by a quick shout or by the use of a whistle. By halting play at a vital moment the coach is able to highlight an aspect of the game that requires attention; the coach and players now have a clear, realistic match situation for all to see and build upon. The coach can either direct the players towards set solutions to overcome the problems identified by the situation or he can get them involved more fully in the learning process by asking them questions which force them to think the problem through and to come up with the solutions themselves. This will reinforce their reading of the game. To avoid any confusion amongst any of the players, the coach could walk certain players over the runs they should make. This slow-motion action replay will clarify for all exactly what is needed.

3.1 FREEZE PLAY – INDIVIDUAL

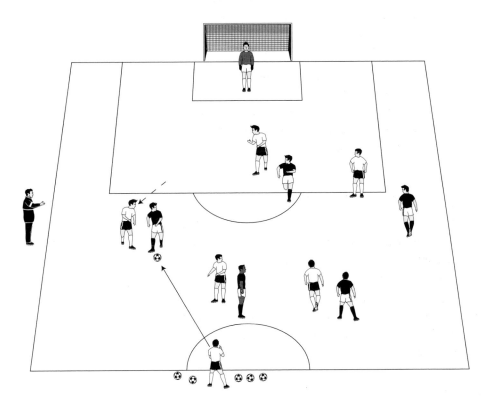

In this example, the coach has frozen play on the right side of the field to isolate the poor challenging position of the nearest defender to the ball. The coach in these circumstances is using the method to work on an *individual* player.

3.2 FREEZE PLAY – TEAM

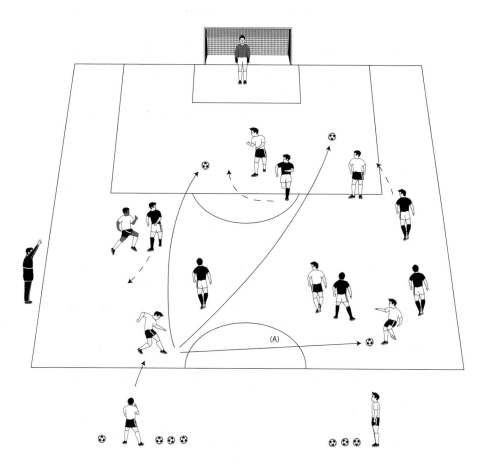

Here, the coach has frozen play to highlight a situation where the attacker with the ball has passed it across the field to a team-mate (A). The coach now has the opportunity to work with him plus his other team-mates and encourage more penetrative passing options and forward running off-the-ball. In this way, he is using the method to work with the *team*.

Advantages

1. The situation in question is conveyed clearly to all.
2. There is a good opportunity for the coach to create a positive visual demonstration.
3. The coach can ask players questions that will enhance communication.
4. The coach can involve players in solving their own problems, therefore increasing their learning and confidence.
5 By involving more players, game-understanding and teamwork can be improved.

Disadvantages

1. If over-used, it will disrupt the practice flow and become frustrating to the players.
2. Players can become physically uncomfortable – especially in cold or wet weather.
3. The coach needs to ensure that he freezes the practice at the critical time and to make sure the players do likewise. If not, the situation created will lack realism. The timing of knowing **when** to stop play will come with practice and experience.
4. The practice can get bogged-down if there is too much discussion between coach and players over alternatives to each situation. When asking questions, keep the responses short and follow quickly with action.
5. As coach ensure that you recreate situations accurately otherwise disagreements can occur. You can lose credibility with the players if you do not get the basic facts correct.

Summary

This method can be effective if used properly at the correct time and if over-use is avoided. When introducing a new tactical idea, it can be used a few times in the early stages to give players a clear picture of it, plus the time to make sense of the tactic and to start to incorporate it into their game. I always tell my players in advance that I will be freezing play once or twice and briefly explain why. This seems to get a better response from them as a result. As a rule, do not use it more than three times during any one practice session.

Method 2 – Condition-play

This method is used to stress a particular aspect of play to the players by repetitive practice so that it becomes conditioned into their game. They can practise techniques, skills or tactics in this way, with or without constantly moving opponents. This narrows the player's choices during the practice so that eventually he can only perform that aspect of play in the game situation. Normally, if the rule or condition is not adhered to in the game (e.g. a player takes three touches of the ball in a two touch game) then a free kick is ordered against the offending team.

A game can be conditioned in four different ways.

1. **By changing the practice area**

   The actual shape or dimensions of the playing space are altered to emphasise a game aspect (e.g. a narrow field to encourage width in attack or a more congested area to promote tighter control and passing of the ball.

2. **By restricting players**

   Certain players can have their movements restricted during play (e.g. defenders must man-mark specific players or certain players are not allowed to tackle).

3. **By changing the rules**

   New rules are introduced to highlight certain techniques, skills or tactics (e.g. the ball must be played under head height or certain players are not allowed to cross the half-way line and must remain in their own half).

4. **By encouraging certain play**

   Players or the team are rewarded if they manage to achieve particular aspects of play. (e.g. headed goals gain an extra goal or every ten consecutive passes equal an extra point).

3.3 CONDITION PLAY – CHANGE PRACTICE AREA

The first way to change your conditioning is to *change your practice area* This practice has 5 v 5 players plus two goalkeepers playing in a more restricted space whilst two wide players play in channels trying to run with the ball and cross to their team-mates who attempt to score. The players who are in the 'inner-field' try to interpass and play the ball out wide to their own player who is unopposed.

3.4 CONDITION PLAY – RESTRICT PLAYERS

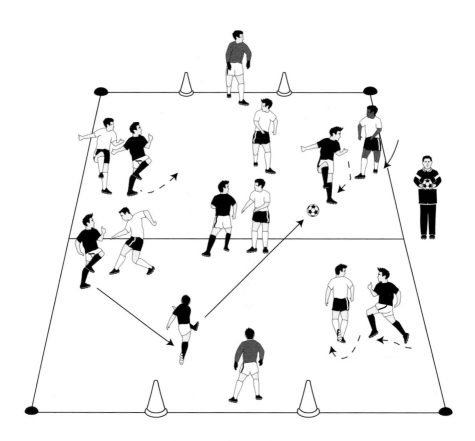

The second way to condition play is to *restrict players*. In this game players are paired-up where they can only mark their own man as they defend. Each team has a sweeper at the back who cannot travel over the halfway line but is restricted to 'two-touch' football and no player is allowed to tackle him. In this way players develop mental discipline in man-marking, and creativity in creating space for themselves when being tightly marked.

3.5 CONDITION PLAY – CHANGE THE RULES

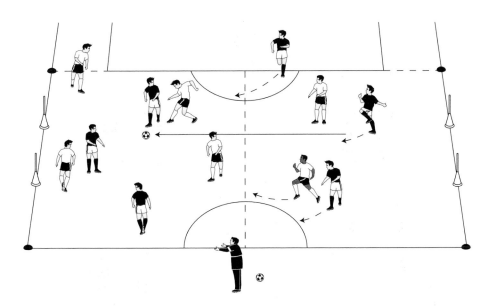

The third way to use conditioning is by *changing the rules*. In this game, a goal is only allowed if the whole team manages to get into the attacking half of the field as the ball crosses the goal line. If the defensive team also fails to get all their players back into their own half, the team that scores is awarded a further goal. This is to work on compact play for both teams.

3.6 CONDITION PLAY – ENCOURAGE CERTAIN PLAY

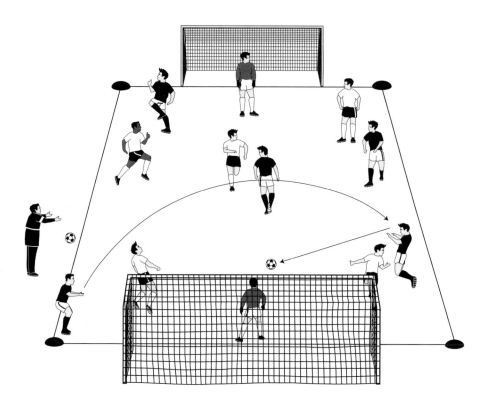

The last way to condition play is to encourage certain play. This game is called 'throw-head-catch' where players are encouraged to practice attacking and defending heading skills.

Advantages

1. The players have opportunity to practise a skill or tactic repeatedly.

2. They can work on an individual weakness in a realistic way.

3. It can aid teamwork as all players work together to make it happen – if not, they are penalised.

4. For the coach, it is easy to organise.

5. It allows all players to focus on one aspect of play considered to be important.

Disadvantages

1. It often needs someone to supervise, if the coach is not available, to ensure that the conditions are enforced.

2. Too much use of this method can narrow the players' thinking by forming bad habits (e.g. over-use of one/two touch in practice can stop a player holding the ball and taking his time where appropriate, etc.).

3. It can be too artificial and loses credibility if care is not taken over its application.

4. It can de-motivate players if over-used – it frustrates them by not allowing them to make their own decisions.

5. It can make both players and team too predictable if used to the extreme – it can destroy their creative instinct.

Summary

This method is used universally by many coaches and can be effective when used correctly. It can emphasise key factors of play to the team; however it is best when used for shortish spells (e.g. 10–15 minutes) and the conditions changed according to the team's needs at the time. The coach must ensure that the conditions are as realistic as possible, that the rules are simple to apply and understand, and that only one condition is used at a time, otherwise confusion will reign. Make players see this method as a challenge, not a restriction to their enjoyment of the game.

Liverpool showed me an ingenious way to retain the flow of the game whilst still using the method. Instead of penalising players who violated the rules (e.g. three touches instead of two etc.) by stopping the game with a free-kick, they allowed them the extra touch and the game to carry on. However, verbal pressure, in a light-hearted way was directed at the player inferring that he did not have the skill to play with the condition. It soon changed players' concentration, attitude and application! There is a lesson here – whatever method you use as a coach, always try to maintain the practice flow as it frustrates players in you do not.

Method 3 – Drillwork

This method involves groups of players practising techniques, skills or tactics from the game, with or without opposition, and where they actively repeat the actions in formation. Some coaches use drills which, although they look busy, do not contribute much to their learning as they are artificial in nature. Other coaches do not like them because they do not believe they replicate realistic situations from the game, so it is better to do all your coaching in game-like situations. Others say the practice game cannot provide all players with the necessary individual repetitive practice they require to build their technical expertise – this needs to be done at times outside the game. As with all coaching, there are no absolutes, each coach must make up his own mind although a large majority use them fairly regularly in some shape or form. To gain the best results, ensure that each drill is realistic, relates to the game and is performed at a reasonably high tempo, just like the actual game. Coaches should not use them in isolation. They must understand how they relate to the whole learning process and integrate them with the other part of the session – usually a game-like situation. They must also ensure that the drill is suitable for the player and that he has the ability, strength and maturity to deal with its demands.

3.7 DRILL – UNOPPOSED

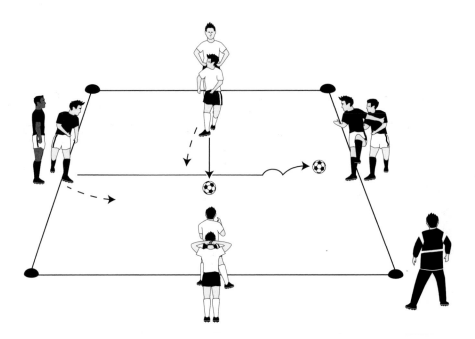

This drill is *unopposed* and is being used to improve passing *techniques*. The cross-information means that players need to pass two footballs almost simultaneously. This involves varied techniques, timing, decision-making and concentration.

3.8 DRILL – OPPOSED

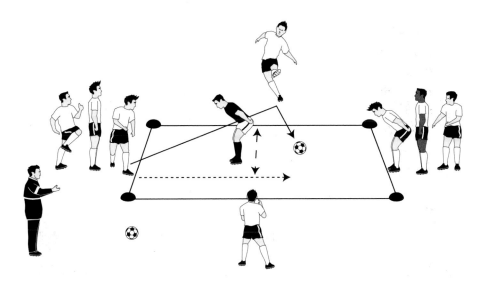

In this example, players are given more realistic *skill* practice in wall-passing. The defender is *semi-active* and can move along central area to intercept the ball. Play continues from end-to-end with the defender turning to face the attackers each time. With added opponents, drills can be designed to develop most skill situations in the game.

Advantages

1. Organisation is normally easy. The coach can effectively involve large groups of players quickly in relevant activities.

2. The coach can change them often to provide variety and motivation for the players.

3. The coach can manipulate the drill complexity, tempo and work-rate to progress.

4. The player has many repetitions of technical skill or tactical moves in a short period.

5. Good activity for pepping-up your warm-up, conditioning work or for short breaks of lighter activities between the more intense practice.

6. Good for rhythm and co-ordination work, especially if used in conjunction with music.

Disadvantages

1. The drills can be artificial. They do not emulate the movement patterns from the real game and can become a circus act.

2. If the drills are too complex, it becomes confusing for the players.

3. If over-used, it can start to narrow the players' thinking and make them predictable.

Summary

Ensure players work at a good tempo and do not use one drill for too long as they will become one-dimensional in their outlook. Remember, it must be used in partnership with the game-situation, not in isolation. Whole-part-whole. Finally, quality should come before quantity – watch the number of players in each group. Too many means lines of players idly standing waiting for their turn whilst not enough will mean that they become fatigued quickly because they have little time to recover between repeating their skills.

Method 4 – Pressure-play

This method needs to be carefully defined as it is often used incorrectly. The coach needs to be sure what exactly it is he wants the player to learn from using this method, as this will determine how he sets the practice up. It can be used to improve individual techniques, decision-making skills or mental reactions. In essence, the players have to contend with fast repetitive delivery of the ball which puts them under pressure – hence the name of the method. There is either a set time period or a set number of repetitions that the player has to contend with. The player has to react quickly and as accurately as possible in order to improve himself. The method is designed to train players to react as fast as they would in a competitive match, especially towards the end of the bout of work when their limbs have become fatigued and heavy, and their mental powers of judgement are beginning to fail. The practice is arranged so that the player(s) receive a continual supply of services from one or more servers, where they have hardly enough time to play the ball before the next one is on its way. The work period or number of services must be estimated and timed so that the player does not work flat-out for longer than 30–45 seconds at a time. The skill factor will begin to suffer if the practice continues for longer than this.

Experience does indicate, however, that many players do not work to their maximum potential during these practices and work periods of up to 60 minutes can be allowed, as long as the service and work periods are controlled. Experienced players with good techniques can do a few bouts of pressure practice consecutively during a session, providing the rest periods are well controlled and allow adequate recovery each time.

3.9 DRILL – INDIVIDUAL UNOPPOSED

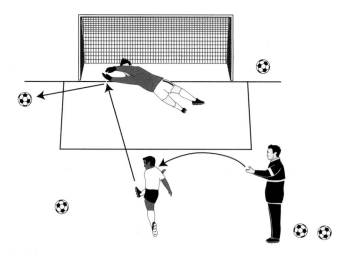

In this example, the coach is working with an *individual* player, the goalkeeper, to improve him with a constant flow of shots on-the-volley from a team-mate. The coach can direct the player to hit one particular type of shot that the goalkeeper needs to practise, or vary the shots. He will develop technique, reaction and concentration with this drill. The method is carried out *unopposed* by other players.

3.10 DRILL – GROUP OPPOSED

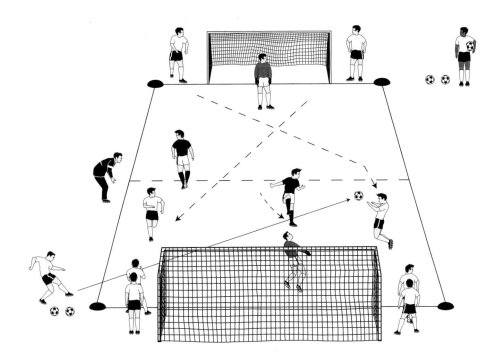

In this drill, two pair of players line up at the sides of two goals placed about 20 yards apart. Two goalkeepers defend the goal whilst two wide players with a good supply of footballs, stand adjacent to each other in wide positions. Two defenders stand in the central area. The drill begins with a pair of attackers using a cross-run to attack the other goal and try to score with a header, volley or knock-down from their team-mate. As soon as they cross the halfway area, one of the defenders runs back to challenge them. Two new attackers run to receive a cross from the other side as the other defender challenges them in turn. The defenders return to the halfway line in turn. The pressure is built-up by the speed, rhythm and complexity of the practice. The method, as you can see, can be used with the *team* and *opposed*.

Advantages

1. For the coach it is relatively easy to organise.

2. The player receives many practice opportunities in a short space of time.

3. The players are usually motivated by the all-action and competitive practice-style.

4. It can help quicken some players' movement, techniques and decision-making skills.

5. It can help players to reproduce techniques when fatigued.

6. The 'overload' principle can be used progressively to improve players' skills.

Disadvantages

1. Never use with players who have poorly developed techniques – they are not ready yet and it will destroy their confidence.

2. If used without thought it can promote bad technical habits in a player who may be unaware of its effect on him.

3. If the service is too fast, slow, inaccurate or predictable, it makes for unrealistic and therefore, poor practice. Needs to be controlled properly.

4. If the service or time period is not controlled, then fatigue can cause technical breakdown and retardation for the future – players need time to recover.

Summary

This method is mainly for individuals; however, units of the team or the whole team itself can undergo pressure work to emulate match conditions. This will help players to rehearse, practise and solidify their technical skills, tactics and match thinking in realistic situations. Young developing players, who do not yet have the techniques, should not be subjected to this method for the reasons already given, although others could be but in a limited way (e.g. shorter time periods, easier techniques and slower timed services). The coach must realise that all players are individuals and will react to pressure differently. Watch for practices that look good but have little transfer of skills into the actual game. Practices should be gradually progressive and as players become more competent, they should be made more difficult. (e.g. more unpredictable services or introduce a defender who is first static, then semi-active and possibly fully active at some stage). The practice must be organised so that the player(s) have some success but are also challenged. -

Method 5 – Shadow-play

This method is one in which a team or unit of a team rehearse some aspect of tactical play or strategy against imaginary opposition. As the practice progresses a few static, semi-static or active opponents who are heavily outnumbered can be introduced in a progressive way to add to the realism of the session. Some coaches find it helps players to develop their system of play and any new tactical innovations that they wish to introduce without the pressure or distraction of opponents. Basically, a team lines up in realistic positions on the field and the ball is fed to any player. The players move and react as if opponents are on the field with them. The coach decides if it is an attacking or defending theme and practice proceeds towards or away from the goal. Often coaches will introduce a condition, such as two-touch, to inject more urgency, a quicker tempo and a more realistic situation.

3.11 SHADOW PLAY – STATIC MODE

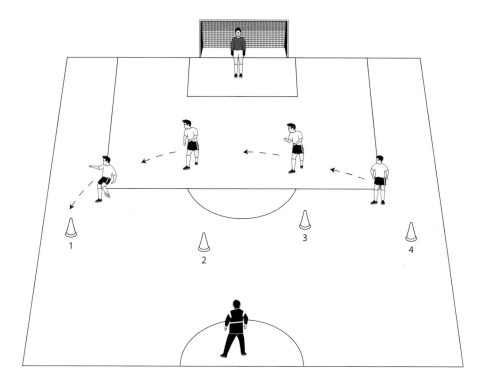

The coach arranges 4 numbered cones across the field. Four players are positioned fairly close together first outside the penalty-area. The coach calls a number – the nearest defender needs to get to his cone quickly (which represents an attacking player) whilst the others take up realistic covering positions. In this way, the defensive play can be choreographed in a *static* fashion so that players can practise defensive-play slowly, repeatedly and systematically.

3.12 SHADOW PLAY – MOVEMENT MODE

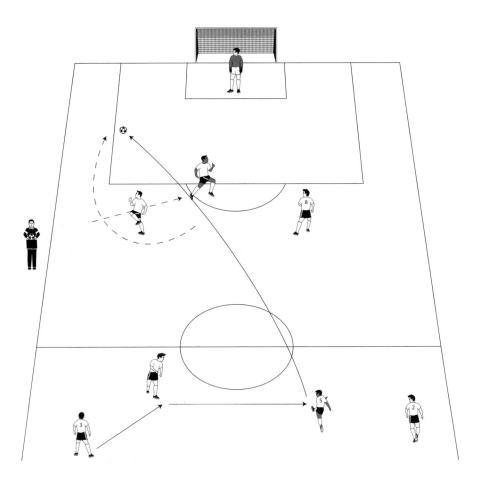

In this example, the back four unit of the team inter-pass until the ball arrives at number 5 the right-sided centre-back. This triggers a set move between two of the front three players on the opposite side of the field. Player 5 plays a long, high pass to coincide with the scissor-run of the attacker who receives the ball bearing-down on goal. Various attacking and defensive combinations can be devised and practiced by various units of the team in this way.

Advantages

1. The aspect of the game to be practised can be seen clearly without distractions.
2. No opponents to hinder players – more freedom to play and less fear.
3. Coach has greater control to get his message across to the players – especially systems of play.
4. Can be good for practising restarts.

Disadvantages

1. Needs much experience, motivation and exhortation at first to make it work.
2. Can create bad habits in practice because of the lack of urgency with no opponents.
3. The lack of opponents can make it unrealistic – some players find it hard to relate to the actual game situation. Needs much imagination.
4. Violates the transfer of training principle – no opponents, therefore hard to measure its effectiveness.

Summary

The coach needs to see that it is as realistic as possible by making runs, reproducing skills and playing at as fast a tempo as normal. A few opponents can be introduced progressively so that the practice can be built up to a more realistic level. This method can prove to be a welcome addition to the coach's tool box, but it does demand much enthusiasm, skill and experience to be effective.

Method 6 – Small-sided games

These games can range from 1 v 1 to 7 v 7 players and can involve odd or even numbers of players. Traditionally, players world-wide first started playing the game as small children on the streets. Each coach has their favourite small games(s) which they can use to get their ideas across to the players in an enjoyable and effective manner. The games can be used and adapted in a variety of ways to provide a number of coaching outcomes.

3.13 SMALL-SIDED – UNOPPOSED

This small game of head-tennis is designed to improve *individual* heading technique in enjoyable and competitive circumstances. The players are *unopposed* and can concentrate on building their techniques without having to think about making body contact with other players – only their own!

3.14 SMALL-SIDED – OPPOSED

Here a circle is marked on the ground and nine players play 6 v 3 with the attackers using their numerical advantage to maintain possession of the ball. The size of the area, its shape, the number of players and the rules of the game can be altered at any time by the coach to improve learning and understanding. The method in this case is *opposed* which will develop skill, decision-making and teamwork.

Advantages

1. The smaller number of players allows for more ball contact and technical skill development.
2. More game involvement and opportunity to learn the basic tactics of the game (e.g. defence and attack).
3. The players have more fun and freedom to express themselves – they become more creative.
4. More physically realistic area for young players – better learning environment.
5. Less complex than full 11 v 11 game – better chance for progressive learning.
6. Easier coaching situation. Fewer players allows for more 'coachable' moments.

Disadvantages

1. It is not like the real thing. Does not always transfer what is learned into the full game situation.
2. Does not develop specific fitness or positions like the 11 v 11 game.
3. Overuse can develop bad habits (e.g. play too much of a short game when playing in the full game).

Summary

This method can be very effective for developing skills and general tactics. The coach can change the rules, shape and dimensions of the playing area or play uneven numbers in one team so they have an advantage over the other. For example, a reduced area will allow more opportunities for dribbling, tackling, ball control and possession play; a longer area will encourage longer passing; place portable goals in a shorter area to encourage shots etc.

Remember, when setting small-sided games, you can adjust the area, numbers and rules to emphasise your coaching theme.

Method 7 – Functional-play

This method concentrates on small units of the team who receive specific coaching on their roles, and the skills and functions needed to play the position. A realistic area of the playing field is marked out and the coach decides whether to concentrate on defence or attack or both. Basically, the player(s) work in the area of the field where they would normally play; the coaching objective is to work with a few players to increase their tactical understanding of what is required.

3.15 FUNCTIONAL PLAY – GOALKEEPING

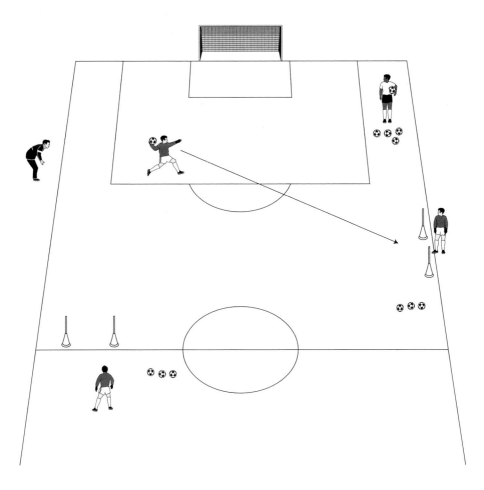

This practice is designed to help the goalkeeper *individually* to function better at distributing the ball to his team. He receives the ball in the air from the wide player before throwing it quickly, smoothly and accurately through the two small targets. The other goalkeepers act as ball retrievers before taking their turn in goal.

3.16 FUNCTIONAL PLAY – ATTACKING

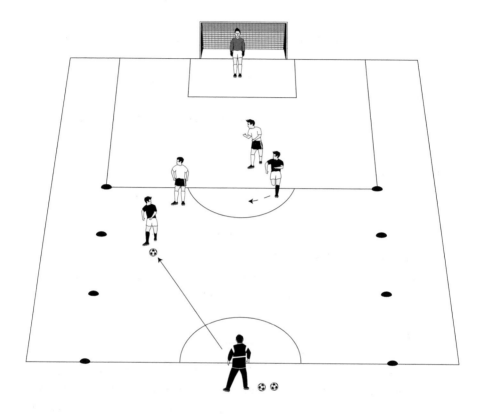

Here, the coach has set up a channel where he can work on his two attackers and how they function as a unit. He can serve them with various passes to produce realistic game situations so they learn how to play together, with and without the ball. The coach in this situation could have decided to work with the centre-backs or he could have marked out appropriate areas on the field to work on other players' functions in the game.

Advantages

1. It can create a rapport between the coach and player because of the individual attention received – this can be highly motivational for learning.
2. Much work can be done to eradicate specific weaknesses in the player.
3. The player can contribute his own ideas – it becomes more player-centred.
4. It can provide fairly realistic, intensive and functional practice to help the player learn his role within the team.

Disadvantages

1. It can be somewhat isolated from the big picture, i.e. the 11 v 11 game.
2. It can provide an organisational headache for the coach – what happens to the other players in the squad?
3. It can drastically show up the weaknesses of some players – need to be aware of this and protect them where possible.

Summary

This method can be effective in helping players' confidence and game understanding by working on weaknesses which may be hindering their development. However, the coach should never forget to stress their strengths in the practices. From a negative point of view, this method's success depends on the motivation and co-operation of all the players involved, which can sometimes be difficult. It also requires a lot of attention from the coach, which can be time-consuming. As soon as players show progress, the practice should be incorporated into a more advanced stage of play involving more players, a greater area of the field and more realistic match-type situations.

Method 8 – Phase-play

This method is a natural progression from the functional method in which the player(s) develop their understanding on the smaller stage before moving onto the larger, more realistic phase of the game. The method aims to develop teamwork and to build up an understanding of its role amongst units of players. The practice is as realistic as can be, with fairly continuous repetitive play at a high tempo. Normally, the coach will concentrate on one phase of play at a time where it is simpler to try to work on attack and defence together. The method can be developed by adding more players and increasing the field area to create realistic match-type situations.

3.17 PHASE-PLAY – ATTACKING (1)

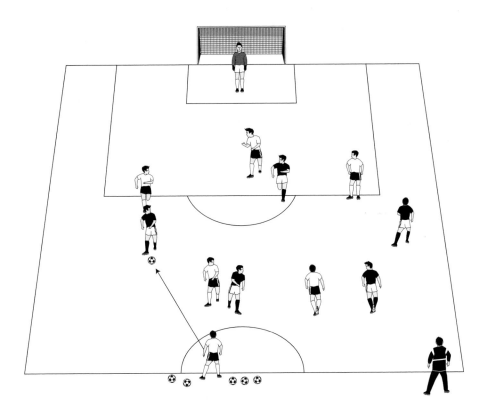

The coach, who previously worked on a functional practice with two attackers, has developed it into a full attacking phase of the game. The two attacking players and others, can begin to see, experience and learn about the more complex environment. This gives them a more realistic bigger picture as they practise.

3.18 PHASE-PLAY – ATTACKING (2)

In this example, the coach is working on an *attacking* phase of the game. The players are aiming to inter-pass smoothly from the back to enter the midfield region with good ball possession. Although the practice is 7 v 7 (not including the goalkeeper), two of the back players A and B can only move along the halfway line. The target for the attackers is for one of them to arrive with the ball at their feet unopposed over the halfway line.

Advantages

1. Good for squad work – gets all players involved.
2. Good for developing teamwork.
3. Good for developing tactical and positional understanding.

Disadvantages

1. Players not directly involved in the practice theme can become bored or de-motivated by feeling left out.
2. Can become too competitive which can affect the learning.
3. Individuals can become 'lost' in the main practice aim of developing team tactical understanding and teamwork.

Summary

This method bridges the gap between the functional and full game methods. The coach can use various methods to get his message across – ensure that you have a few servers at various positions and give clear targets for both attackers and defenders to conclude the practice.

Method 9 – Coaching in full game

Here the coach employs a few of the other coaching methods already mentioned to coach one or both teams in the full 11 v 11 game on a full-sized field. Many coaches feel this is the ultimate coaching situation – the real deal. This method seem to have maximum transfer of training to the full competitive match. It is good for facilitating teamwork, tactical understanding and cementing the system-of-play.

3.19 COACHING – TEAM ORGANISATION

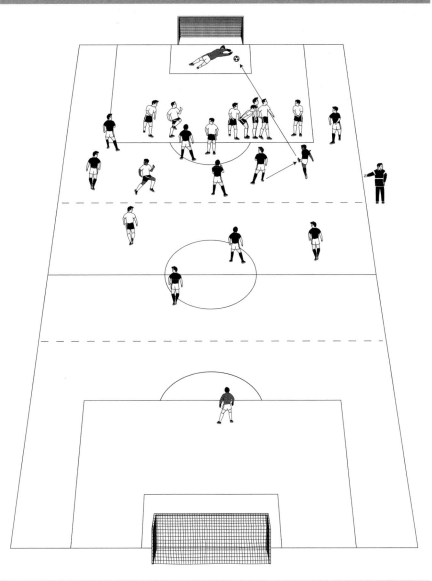

In this example, the coach is working on team organisation and understanding at restarts. By allowing play to flow in the full 11 v 11 game he can blow his whistle like a referee for an imaginary free-kick, corner-kick or throw-in in the various thirds of the field so that defensive or attacking players can take the appropriate action.

3.20 COACHING – TEAM PATTERNS

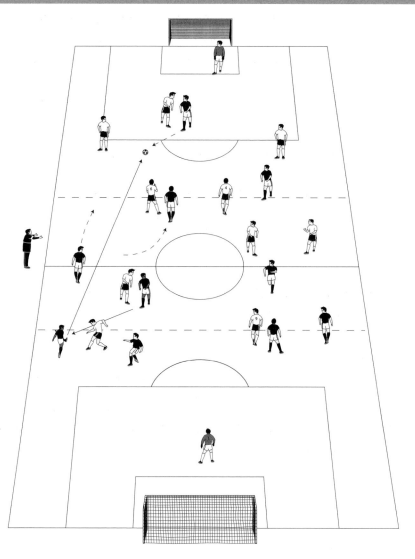

Here the coach can decide to work on set topics of play using different methods for short periods within the 11 v 11 game (e.g. freeze play to highlight situations; conditioned play to encourage longer passes; or shadow-play to rehearse movements, before building back up to 11 v 11. Remember not to over-complicate the situation and always end your session with an *un-coached* game.

Advantages

1. It has a good transfer of training – a realistic learning situation.
2. Good method for teamwork, tactical play and system-of-play.
3. Often players like playing in the full game where the experience is more realistic.

Disadvantages

1. Over-use can start to cause tension and staleness. No chance to switch-off from 11 v 11 in competition or practice, which causes stress.
2. Does not allow individual work – it is all about the team.
3. The games can become over-competitive at times (e.g. first team and reserves) and little learning is achieved.

Summary

This method can be very effective when used by a coach who is confident, comfortable and experienced in its use.

General

These guidelines are designed to assist the coach to organise his practice sessions at the correct level and to help his players receive maximum benefit from his expertise. By developing confidence and knowledge, and by the skilful application of his coaching methods, he can help each player and the team to achieve their maximum potential.

CHAPTER 4
COMMUNICATION WITH THE TEAM

Good communication between the coach and players is vital to the team's success. A coach spends much of his time passing on ideas and information to players; if he fails to communicate effectively confusion and frustration for everyone results. He must remember that each player is different and his approach must cater for this. For example, some players will respond to a quiet, friendly and persuasive approach, while others will react better to a firm, no-nonsense set of directions.

PRINCIPLES OF COMMUNICATION

1. **Understand the message**

   Coaches often think that because they have told players something, they will understand what is wanted. This is not always so, as players vary in their capacity to receive, interpret and memorise information. He must see that his message is fully understood by all his players. He must use simple words – and as few as possible – and must avoid too much jargon, which may confuse players. Players who do not fully understand what has been discussed should see him individually for further explanation and clarification. But this can only happen if he encourages players to approach him and doesn't frighten them.

2. Positive instruction

Coaches must always be clear and positive when talking to players, never depressing, defeatist or unclear about the situation. It is no use continually telling a player or team that they are doing something wrong without telling them why they are doing it wrong and how they can correct it. For example, a coach who informs a player that he has passed a bad ball is not telling the player anything he does not know already; but informing him that he hit a bad pass because he hit a ball at the wrong time or to the wrong team-mate is much more positive and helps the player to improve. This does not mean that players should not be criticised; they should, but criticism should be constructive. The coach of an English league club once told me that you should never say to a player or team, 'see how it goes' before a match, as this reflects a lack of confidence in what you are doing. Be positive!

3. Player involvement

Communication between the coach and players where questions and ideas are shared is generally very productive. Encouraging players to discuss matters will add to their knowledge of the game and motivate them to improve their play. The more questions a coach can answer well, the more respect he will gain from his players; however, he should never pretend he knows the answer to a question when he does not. It is more honest to say that you do not know and ask if any other player knows the answer. If he does, give him full credit; however, if no-one knows, inform the players that you will find out from other sources as soon as possible. The danger of discussion is that players talk too much and ask negative or illogical questions; in these circumstances the coach must instruct such players to communicate in a more direct manner and stick to the point.

METHODS OF COMMUNICATION

There are several methods of communication that the coach can employ with his players, but these must take into consideration such factors as the personality of the player, the reason for communicating with the player and what the aim is, and the best place in the circumstances to talk to the player (e.g. the training area, the coach's office, the dressing room).

The command

A coach must be clear and precise with his instructions, telling the player exactly what he should do. For example, he might say to a player who is giving his opponent too much room, 'I want you to get closer to the attacker and stop him turning with the ball'. This method is effective when time is short and players need quick and simple information, say at half-time, or when there is a need for urgent instruction.

The discussion

There must be effective dialogue between the coach and players so efficiency and performance can be improved. This can be achieved through relaxed discussion where both sides can air their views freely. Often a player will open up more than he would in a formal team talk where the atmosphere is slightly inhibiting. Players who are shy or lack confidence can be helped to overcome this in two ways: by asking questions and by challenging players.

The coach asks players for their ideas and suggestions on overcoming specific problems. This stimulates players to think for themselves and allows them to find solutions for themselves rather than always having to depend on the coach. Coaches must learn to ask open-ended questions which promote good communication with the players.

Another technique is to challenge the players to find answers to problems. For example: 'Let's see if you can break down this packed defence' or 'There's no way you can score more goals from that re-start – is there?' The coach must ensure that the objective does not stray too far from its original intent, and that it is kept on track to overcome the problem.

The team talk

More serious and immediate matters are relayed to the players by the coach in the team talk: a one-way system with little interruption. The team talk can cover anything from team discipline to tactical preparation for a forthcoming match.

The tone of the voice and topic should vary according to the needs of the moment and the objective. Often team talks are ill prepared and fail to reach the conclusions that were hoped for. They need to be planned in advance with much thought given to approach, style and content; things can begin to go wrong if the meeting is not organised correctly.

Match analysis

The coach can give factual and objective information to players by analysing and explaining details about their performance. This must be handled carefully as some players may feel threatened if they take this as a personal criticism. He must persuade and assure his players that it is being done to improve individual and team performance. He should analyse parts involving a large number of players (e.g. midfield or back four) where faults can be shown clearly to the team without individuals being identified and where they can see what needs improving without being shown up in front of their team-mates. If he wants to show an individual player a fault, the coach must do so in a sensitive and positive way – sometimes individually.

Visual demonstration

The coach can communicate information and ideas with visual aids and demonstration in a variety of ways. A bright and well-designed notice-board can be the focal point in the dressing room and can display up-to-date information such as training schedules, match reports, travel arrangements for away matches, and team meetings. Films or video tapes of matches played can also be valuable in allowing players to see the good or bad parts of their performance. The coach can also communicate ideas by setting up demonstrations for players and discussing items from them.

Match communication

It is important that players give each other reliable information quickly during the match. This can help the play and team organisation. Often the goalkeeper or the players at the back are in a better position to see what is happening and thus able to call to a team-mate to take appropriate action. A considerable number of goals are given away because one or more defenders fail to communicate properly. How many times do we see an attacker sneaking in to score a goal while defenders argue about who should mark an attacker to prevent him scoring? The coach must spend some time during practice making sure all players are familiar with the terms to use when calling to each other, and that they call clearly, at the correct time, and in a positive and constructive way. Signals familiar to all the players can be used at re-starts to indicate which routine will be used – 'an early shout sorts it out'. He must ensure all players learn to communicate effectively with each other during the match – a time when it is easy to lose one's nerve.

GETTING YOUR MESSAGE ACROSS

Speak effectively

A coach's job requires him to communicate verbally with players, other staff members, and often the media. Some, although good at talking to players in their own environment of the dressing room and playing field, do not come over well in the media. They could improve their methods of communication by critical analysis of their speech, choice of words, and the style and delivery used.

How to speak is important in your relationship with players; words affect the way players react so the coach needs to give thought to his vocabulary. How he feels about coaching will be reflected by how he speaks about it (e.g. cynical coaches will speak negatively). Speech should be simple, logical and clear; the coach should use few words and use terms that will be understood by all the players. Positive instructions must be given which will inspire players to want to improve – avoid negative statements such as bad pass. Indeed, a player must be told why he made a bad pass and how he can make a good one. The voice should be used for effect, for example, talking quickly to show enthusiasm, low and emotionally to 'fire up' the team for a match or loudly to emphasise a point. Important sentences should be repeated for emphasis, but bad habits in speech must be avoided. Coaches should talk directly and clearly to the players, ensuring they do not mumble. Some coaches are excellent communicators – others could do with a little more practice!

Where to talk

Players will be less receptive to a talk if the circumstances are wrong. Often the coach will talk to players on the training area or pitch after they have been involved in a hard physical session, when they are fatigued both mentally and physically; or else they will try to gain players' attention when they are sitting down and cooling off after work. Talking to players in these situations, or above the noise in the dressing room, is a waste of breath. The coach should wait until the players have showered and cooled down, or at least until they are in a reasonably receptive state. Often the worst time is just after a match when the team has lost, or in your office where they may be defensive.

Where to stand

The coach must ensure that he stands where every player can see and hear him clearly, with the wind at his back if talking to the players in the open so that his voice will carry to them. It is a good idea to try to make sure that the sun is not shining directly into the players' or the coach's eyes as this can be very distracting. There can be a number of distractions which can affect the quality of your communication either indoors or out, therefore make sure your position does not add to them.

THE MEDIA

Press, radio and television can be very useful for promoting the players and the club, but there are also dangers involved; some reporters seem to be more interested in the sensational issues rather than the routine ones involving the everyday running of the club. The coach must be careful when making statements to the press, particularly after a poor team performance when he may be angry, in case he says something he regrets later. He should try to build up a rapport with the local media and co-operate as far as possible with their representatives, because not only can he communicate current information about the team to the public, but he can also help his players by editing match reports and after-match statements. These can indirectly communicate his ideas and give praise or criticism to individual team members. Statements made by him after the game should be carefully thought out and worded to avoid any misunderstandings. As a general rule he must avoid criticising individual players in public – he could talk about play in general or even units of the team, but to talk about a player in public could alienate him permanently. It is far better to see the player on his own later to discuss his performance. Never criticise a player or team in public that you are soon to meet – it will probably motivate them to try that much harder against your own team! When talking to pressmen before a match, continental coaches are masters of playing down their team's chances. This is psychologically sound, as it helps give the opposition a false sense of security and thus takes some pressure away from the coach's team.

The coach can write a match report for the local press or for radio which can convey things such as concern about, satisfaction with, anger at or support for the team's display and current form. This can be an important medium for communicating with the players at any level – from schoolboy to top professional. The modern coach needs to come to terms with the media for he will be called upon to communicate with them often; this means becoming skilful at dealing with television, radio and giving interviews to the press.

IMPROVING YOUR COMMUNICATION

The coach has a vital role at his club in developing and maintaining positive communication between different people, whether they are fans, players, staff, or members of the Board of Directors. Here are some guidelines.

Face-to-face conversations

Often the coach does not have a great deal of time, but where he can he should chat to individuals or groups of players at every opportunity. For example, these may be private interviews or discussions in the office, encounters in the corridor or dressing room, or talks with the players on the club coach travelling to and from a match. These 'give and take' talks present an excellent opportunity for exchanging confidences and can help to build trust between the coach and the player. It is very important, even when angry at a player's attitude and behaviour, that he never uses any information gained during these conversations against the player, otherwise word will get around the team that he repeats things said to him in confidence. Often coaches are not very good at communicating in this fashion, preferring to talk to the team as a whole. One-on-one conversations are very important to building up sound communication, however, and should be used at every opportunity even if it is merely small talk.

Get to know your players

Coaches must not treat players merely as units in the team. They should get to know each player personally, finding out as much background information as possible – information that may directly or indirectly affect the player's performance and potential. This may include the player's relationship with his parents and family, his objectives in life and in the game, his school and academic work, his heroes, his general likes and dislikes, and his interests. He must not interrogate the player; any talk of this kind should be in a relaxed atmosphere, for example when a player is giving his background details for filling in a form. The idea is to get a general understanding of the player and the environment from which he comes. A player who comes from a deprived background is likely to have a different approach and objectives to a player who has come from a secure one. All information gained in this way must be kept completely confidential by the coach otherwise he may lose the player's trust. Soccer is unfortunately full of mistrust and suspicion about peoples' motives; therefore the need to show genuine interest in the player is essential.

Listening to players

For coaches to become good communicators, they must first learn to become good listeners. Failing to listen to players will lose them many chances to build up trust and learn about the individual team member. They should listen to what the player is saying without being impatient and interrupting – and should then demonstrate that they have understood. In this way they will gain the players' respect and ensure better communication.

Communication will be enhanced if the coach adopts an 'open door' policy, where the players feel free to talk to him confidentially at any time about any subject that may be bothering them. He cannot expect commitment from a player if he has no time to listen to him. Take time to listen to players when you can – it will pay big dividends in a number of ways.

Body language feedback

The coach can learn to 'read' players just as he has learnt to read the game, by becoming aware of and understanding how they are reacting and feeling about club matters. The problem is that a player may say that everything is alright, disguising his real feeling that everything is all wrong. In this case, the coach can learn by identifying and interpreting body signals, which will give him information about the player's present state of mind. Some coaches are very intuitive and can read signs naturally, but all can become better at this with practice. For example, the face can give away fear, surprise, joy and anger; players can show negative reactions to the coach's words by frowning and narrowing the eyes, or stifling a yawn, or by showing no facial expression at all. A player may turn away from him and avoid looking as he speaks or may sit hunched tensely in a chair. There is a considerable amount of literature available on the science of body language which can help him to understand more about the attitude of the players.

All too often there is a difference between what coaches *think* they have said to players and what they have *actually* said, and between how they feel they have approached the situation and how the player feels he has been treated. Often, a misunderstanding occurs between the intended and the actual action and results in a barrier between the coach and the player; this is usually temporary and easily resolved, but it can sometimes be permanent. In a sport such as soccer it is inevitable that communication problems will arise. For example, instructions may have been unrealistic or were not heard properly in the excitement of the dressing room before a match; a highly-sensitive player may take offence to a particular remark, or a player's or coach's attitude may be coloured by prejudice, jealousy or frustration. The coach must be aware that certain words and the emotional way in which they are used may have a strong influence on certain players and virtually none on others. He must consider what he says and how he says it, as even the most innocent speech can be misunderstood. This is because players have been conditioned in the use of certain words or phrases which make them feel degraded, angry, ridiculed or fearful.

TEAM TALKS

The coach spends a considerable amount of his time talking to his players in both a formal and informal way. The communication cycle illustrated below suggests a way to approach a match.

TEAM TALKS The team manager spends a considerable chunk of his time talking to his players in both a formal and informal way. The communication cycle illustrated suggests a way to approach a match

Pre-match tactical talk

This is best done at least two hours before the match, when the players are still fairly receptive (unlike immediately before the match when excitement and tension are high). Usually the opponent's strengths and possible weaknesses are analysed and assessed as individuals and as a team. Players should be encouraged to ask and discuss anything that is not clear to them – the coach should make sure that each player fully understands his role in the team and exactly what his responsibilities are in the match. Any points of disagreement have to be sorted out at this stage. It is better if some scouting of the opposition has been done beforehand, as it gives players confidence to know what they are likely to be facing. However, he must be careful how he presents the information on the opposition; he should not make them appear unbeatable! He ought to reassure the team that if they perform their roles correctly and stick to the team plan, they have nothing to fear and stand a good chance of winning. The tactical talk should not last too long and it should be clear and simple. It is hard for players to concentrate effectively for longer than 40 minutes.

Pre-match pep talk

This is often badly executed by coaches, mainly through lack of thought or conviction. An effective pep talk must be fresh and inspirational, and the approach must be changed when needed. Often coaches give repetitive pep talks week after week and try to cram too much last-minute information. This is wrong because players are already under considerable pressure at the time and are unreceptive to all but the simplest information. The pep talk is essentially a 'stimulator' to encourage players to do their best in the match. It is often best given in an emotional way as this is usually what inspires players at this stage. He must decide whether the players are too 'high' or too 'low' and temper his pep talk accordingly. Some players will need calming down, while others will need boosting.

The pep talk must cater for individuals as well as the team. It is best to sit down beside a player as he is getting changed and talk quickly and quietly to him about the key points. Some coaches feel uncomfortable about approaching their players before a match, but they have no reason to be – players expect it as it supports them. He should never mention a player's weaknesses before the game as it is likely to lower his confidence. He should talk positively about his strengths and tell him how well he is going to do. For example, if a player is a good dribbler tell him so and tell him to take on defenders. Coaches are often anxious about the outcome of a game and can transmit their anxiety to the players by their talk and manner. For example, I have heard coaches (myself included) say to a goalkeeper who has lost a few 'soft' goals over the last month, things like, 'Watch the crosses today' or 'Remember to go for everything in the air but make sure you get there'. Players are at their most vulnerable just before a competitive game so care is needed – be positive!

Half-time talk

This talk by the coach is a mixture of tactical direction and stimulus. During this period he must get the players' full attention. He should try to get through to the players who present a possible threat to the team performance and support them as the situation demands. The more reliable performers generally do not need this, so time can be spent on those who do. He must keep control of his emotions and must use every minute effectively by getting directly to the point. He must think clearly and objectively about what is going wrong with the individuals and the team, and what he is going to say and do to put it right. He should never let his anger and disappointment influence his analysis and objectivity. He must make the players listen and make sure his points get across to them. The worst mistake is to tell the team it is doing well at half-time! The players will often consciously or subconsciously relax – in these circumstances he must try to find them a new target to aim for. There are two games – one in each half. The players have completed a game, now it is a new one.

Talks at half-time include predictions of what the coach thinks will happen in the second half, based largely on what has happened in the first, but players must be prepared to adapt their tactics on the field should these predictions prove to be incorrect. Much will depend on the result or how the team is performing. It may be a crisis situation where the team needs to be jolted out of its lethargy, or the players may need stimulation and support to keep doing what they have done for the first 45 minutes. It may require tactical changes, the introduction of new blood (substitutions), or an assessment of whether a slightly injured player can last the match; the coach needs to make effective use of the short time available to communicate with impact.

Match inquest

Some coaches take their anger out on players after a game by locking dressing room doors and subjecting the team to verbal abuse or anger after they have performed poorly. The dressing room is a potentially explosive place after a defeat and he is usually in a better position to speak to the players after he and the players have had time to cool off!

Players and coaches are still under a certain amount of emotional pressure after the excitement of a match, whatever the result. If the team has done well, it should be congratulated, but not excessively – the coach must remember that his preparation for the next game is beginning and the players must keep their feet on the ground. He should not criticise players or the team until they have cooled down. Players must be approached, if at all, depending on their personality and how they have played – if they have played badly, they are likely to be on their guard. If they are 'cocky' and have played well, they should be told that they have done 'all right' and players who have tried hard but had a poor game should be supported. Occasionally, when the team has played very badly because of lack of effort and poor attitude, then the coach can 'have a go' verbally, immediately after the match. This can be done for two reasons – it can release emotional anger from the coach and it will let players know in no uncertain terms that things will have to change in their performance.

The debriefing is therefore best undertaken a few days after the match – usually before the first training session and after the players have spent the weekend relaxing and thinking about their personal performance and contribution to the result. Remember, it is always easier to deal with a win – the test of a coach will be when his team loses. This is the time when he should begin a damage limitation exercise and look for positive things to salvage and build upon from the match. Not easy, but possible!

COMMUNICATION BLOCKS

Over talking

Almost all coaches are guilty of this at some time. They should not use too many words, and the ones that they do use should be simple and easily understood. He must get to the heart of the matter and stick to the point. Players will quickly lose interest if you talk too much, so say what you want to say in the easiest, clearest way possible.

Speaking habits

All coaches have certain peculiarities which block effective communication, such as repeating themselves, mumbling, using phrases such as 'you know', or turning away from players as they speak to them. Other bad habits include putting their hands up by their mouth when speaking, or talking too quickly. They must look at players and speak directly to them in a simple and clear fashion. Bad habits tend to switch players off to what you want to get across to them, so be aware of such habits and their effects.

Illogical speaking

Coaches must ensure that they present their information logically, talking the players through the various stages so they understand the topic fully, before moving on to more difficult areas. Some jump from one area to another; they should be systematic and orderly, so that their theme can be developed properly logically.

When discussing intricate tactics, he must start from the basics and wait until the concepts are fully understood and ingrained before moving on to the more complex elements – simple but not always done!

DEFENCE MECHANISMS

We all have these to call upon when we feel threatened or likely to be exposed as having some sort of weakness. The coach must realise that there may be hidden agendas in a player's mind of which he has no knowledge. For example, he may realise that although talking reasonably to a player, he is not getting through to him. The player may still be harbouring a grudge after being dropped from the team a few weeks before. Often there are misunderstandings which could be resolved if brought up and discussed – hence the need for open communication. Often, he will think he is communicating with his players when in fact he is not. These blocks are sometimes difficult to spot, but the following guidelines will help.

Question players

The coach can interrupt his talk and ask his players at random, or in particular the ones he thinks are not paying attention, to repeat what he has been talking about. He must be subtle and not let players feel like they are being ridiculed. For example, he might say to a player, 'Well, Ian, what do you think of that idea?' If the player does not answer satisfactorily, he can use a 'questioning' facial expression which lets the group know that they must concentrate on the information he is giving them; the player is reminded to listen. If the players feel they might be asked their opinion, it keeps them on their toes.

Signs from players

The coach can learn much from looking at the movement and manner of players when talking to them, as everyone exhibits general and specific peculiarities. Uncooperative players can develop signs such as standing at a further distance from him than usual or moving away as he is talking. Often, players show defensive signs, such as crossing their arms across their chests, looking away from the coach as he speaks, drawing an imaginary line with their feet between themselves and him as he is speaking, yawning, shuffling their feet, or refusing to get involved in conversation even when he tries hard to start a discussion. Signs like these can be interpreted easily and clearly – he must change his talk to regain attention.

Summary

The coach is often heavily involved with his players and so he will be communicating with them at individual and team level in a variety of ways. He must seek to improve his own communication abilities to the fullest extent by paying attention to the established principles of good communication – his job will largely depend on it.

CHAPTER 5
TEAM BUILDING

When a coach joins a new club, his terms of reference and responsibilities must be made clear by the Board or Committee which has appointed him. Problems between him and the Board over such things as team selection, cash and expenditure, and general procedure, often emerge later in the season. It is essential to establish clearly from the start what the responsibilities of the coach are, especially over building the team. How far is the Board prepared to go to gain success and what do they expect? For example, it may want a stable, happy, though relatively unambitious club where the family atmosphere is all-important, rather than one which is highly ambitious and competitive. Whichever it is, the coach should know what is required, because it may mean the difference between deciding to tear the team apart and allowing several players to leave the club, or keeping the existing players and building the team from that base. Once he knows the objectives of the Board, he can decide whether or not the job is for him. The following factors are relevant to building the team.

Player recruitment

In the world of professional soccer the problems of player recruitment have become a nightmare for many coaches because of the ever-increasing transfer fee demands. The freedom to buy is determined by the amount of cash available, and the pressure on him at this stage is immense as he has to decide whether or not the player is worth the asking price. At whatever level of the game he is involved, whether he decides that the team needs the addition of just one or two players or that it requires major surgery and the departure of several players, the coach is responsible for re-building the team. He will have his own ideas about the type of player he favours and the tactics he wishes to employ, but he should first take stock of the entire situation and assess what positions need strengthening and who needs replacing in the squad.

Gradual change

The coach who comes to a club and immediately sets about transforming it provokes hostility from the players. He should study the players and the team, assess what needs to be done, and resolve to do it gradually. Patience is needed to tolerate those players who may not form part of his long-term plans. He may find that players who have not performed near their maximum for some time only needed the stimulus of a change of coach to bring out their full potential. Sometimes a suggestion that the player should change position helps him to become more successful and thus an asset to the team. The coach may introduce new tactics, new training routines or new approaches in general, all of which have the effect of improving performance.

The close season is the ideal time to make new signings and introduce them to the other players, the training routine and the style of team play. However, from time to time situations may arise in which the coach has to take decisive action with immediate effect, for example, when players have been at the club for a long time and formed themselves into cliques, which have worked to manipulate or influence other players in a negative way. If he can identify these players and make it clear that he is not going to tolerate such factions within his club, then he may gain respect and make a good impact on the remaining players, who in turn, may settle down and use their playing ability to the club's fullest advantage.

Scouting system

Once a coach decides that new players are necessary, his next problem is to locate the right ones and persuade them to join his club. It is not easy to do this at any level of the game, but it is certainly much more difficult at the professional level where large sums of money are involved. There are various ways of finding new players: individuals can scout and attend matches in an organised sequence so that most players and teams in the league can be observed; players can be taken on a loan period at the club where appropriate; or trial matches can be arranged to spot promising young players. It is vital to know which players are available and how they play. A coach will know the type of player he is looking for in terms of technique, skill, and physical and tactical abilities, but he will also want to know something of his character and personality.

When considering a new player for his club, a coach must ensure that he will fit in and not cause trouble through his personality or behaviour. Some form of investigation needs to be made, especially if he has not seen the player in action very often. He can ask an ex-coach for his opinion, or ask players from his own team who may have played with or against the player, or even consult a member of the press who may have followed the player's career to date. One English league club has been known to employ a private investigator to uncover information about a player! This may be going too far, but it is important to make thorough enquiries. Most professional clubs also give any potential recruit a thorough medical test to assess his physical fitness. Therefore, if a coach does his homework properly he will know where any likely problems with a new player might lie and be prepared for all eventualities.

Settling in period

The coach must realise that it is often difficult for a newcomer to settle in to his new club. He needs time to get used to his new team-mates, tactics, team manger, coach, training and coaching routines as well as a new environment. Patience is needed, especially if the player is recruited mid-season or if the team is going through a bad time. Often the player is thrown in at the deep end and expected to perform miracles, when he should be allowed to settle in gradually. He will often be assessed rather critically by the coach, supporters, Board and his fellow players as soon as he is signed and therefore has to earn their respect very quickly.

There are several ways in which a coach can help the newcomer to cope with this immediate pressure. He could take the new player with him to watch the team, so that he can see how they play and how his own style will fit in. Tactical sessions could be set up so that the new player can familiarise himself with the pattern of play and his role in the team. The supporters could be asked through the local newspaper to welcome and encourage the newcomer. Much will depend on the experience of the new signing; he may want to play immediately or it may be better to allow him time to adjust to the new conditions, especially if the player comes from another country.

Taking over a new team

When taking over a new team, the coach must not be too hasty to carry out changes. A period of adjustment is necessary so that he and the team can get to know each other, while the past experience of the players and the club must be taken into account.

The coach is bound to be compared with his predecessor and there may be an initial degree of mistrust or confusion which has nothing to do with him personally but which nevertheless has to be overcome. It is essential to achieve some early success with the squad, whether training, coaching, tactically or psychologically. It is best to select areas where it is relatively easy to attain success – this will win the players' confidence.

The coach needs to analyse his entire playing staff over a period of time before deciding on his approach to them and to the squad as a whole. For example, some players may be negative in their approach so a firm line is needed, or the team may be on a losing run and as a result be demoralised. It then requires patience to build them up to the required level of confidence.

Coaches change clubs regularly and some do better at one club than they do at another. When taking over a new club, he must find out exactly what his duties will be to prevent misunderstandings at a later date. He must also find out as much about the club as he can – its traditions, style of play and image, as they affect players, staff, ground, etc. The coach must beware of accepting negative information about certain players, which gives him a pre-conceived idea of their character and affects his attitude to them. Often, players who have been out of favour and a problem to the old coach can hit it off with the new one and find success. Ideally, it is best to take over a new club towards the end of the season, as this allows a coach time to assess fully the strengths and weaknesses of the players, their style of play, the facilities and the existing training programme. He can then start to correct faults, bring in new players and allow others to go, and gradually put his ideas into practice in preparation for the following season.

Breaking up the team

After assessing the squad over a period of time the coach may feel, for various reasons, his players are not compatible and may decide to release many of them and break up the team. The longer he has been at the club the more difficult this will be, as he will have formed friendships with players and will have to tell them that they are no longer needed. It is best to make the transition gradually by introducing new players into the squad in a sensible way. Some clubs have an excellent record for producing successful teams over the years, thus maintaining consistency. Some coaches have failed to see the inevitable and have allowed veteran and ex-star players to go on playing without making provision for their eventual decline by giving younger players the necessary match experience. Timing the introduction of new players is very important, as players who stay at a club too long can become complacent and can block the progress of up-and-coming youngsters at the club who need experience.

The more success the club has had in the immediate past and the bigger the names of the players concerned, the greater the pressure on the team manager to keep players who may be past their best. Breaking up the team requires insight, clarity and courage.

CHANGING THE STYLE OF PLAY

The fear of losing runs through almost every level of the game. Soccer has become more competitive and the need to win is therefore more pressing. All coaches love to win, however some are more concerned about not losing and so adopt a safe and cautious defensive approach with their team; others attempt to play artistic soccer and regularly lose. The coach must be realistic when changing the team's style of play and consider the short-term needs of the club as well as the long-term ones. For example, he may join a club towards the end of a season to try to save it from being relegated to a lower division and he may decide that the team needs to alter their style of play to be more defensive/attacking; this may involve a change of players' roles. He needs to be careful about this as players usually require time to adapt and older players may find it more difficult. When deciding to change the team's style of play, the following points should be considered.

The present situation

The coach must consider whether the climate is right for a change and, if so, when to implement this. For example, the team could find themselves heading for relegation or they could have hit a sudden loss of form when poised for promotion. Should the coach wait for the return of the previously successful style, or should a change be made immediately? The players, the fans and even the coach may be getting depressed and disillusioned with the old ways and need the fresh stimulus of a new, more vibrant approach.

Team characters

What are the players like as individuals and how do they interact with one another? Although each player has his own characteristics, the team will have a general character of its own, shaped by the stronger personalities. Older players may be conservative in their thinking, set in their ways and resistant to change; on the other hand, they could be very loyal to the coach and give any changes a chance to work, especially if they seem to aid their own, or the team's, performance.

Team ability

The coach must consider the technical skill, physical fitness and tactical understanding of the individuals in the squad before changing the style of play. For example, if he wishes to change the defensive style of play from a zonal-marking role to one where attackers are marked tightly man-for-man for the duration of the game, then he needs to be sure that the defenders in question are physically able to cope with the extra running load; if he wishes his defensive-based rear players to attack more often, he must be sure that they have the necessary technical ability and skill to do so. He must not give them tasks beyond their ability.

The coach must emphasise the following three factors when implementing changes to the style of play.

1. **The benefits**

    The coach must make players see the need for change and persuade them that they will benefit personally from this. The main difficulty in changing an individual's style of play is that over the years he will have picked up habits, both good and bad. Persuading older players that the new style will be better is also often difficult and requires patience. However, one thing is clear – if he wants to change the team's style of play, the manager must change the individuals within that team and show them benefits.

2. **Be patient**

    Any changes should be made gradually. If they are made too quickly, or if too many players are changed at once, confusion will ensue. For example, coaches have been known to change a team suddenly whose style has been organised on defence into a creative all-out attacking one, often informing the players in the dressing room just before the match starts! Players cannot be expected to cope with this sudden variation in style, which means abandoning time-honoured methods, a few minutes before the heat and emotional excitement of a competitive match. Before a team changes its style of play there should be much discussion, practice, coaching, and general preparation to familiarise the players with the new style before it becomes fully integrated.

3. **Play to strengths**

   Players should never be asked to perform skills they are not capable of – weaknesses must be camouflaged, not exploited, for the team's benefit. Some coaches have an irrational fondness for a particular system and will try to select players to fit that system. He must be realistic when changing the style of play of the team; it is unrealistic to expect a winger who is known for his creative ability to spend almost the entire game defending and tackling. Players must be used on the side of the field where they feel most comfortable and where they can use their strengths. It may even be necessary to stop players playing the ball to team-mates in positions where their limitations may be exposed; for example, the goalkeeper may be instructed not to throw the ball out to a particular full back on his team who has poor ball control for fear that he will lose possession to the opposition in a dangerous position near his goal. Conditioned games are good for promoting this idea.

As far as changing to a new playing system is concerned, you should either try one system with different players or different systems with the same players. Too much chopping and changing threatens players; always make sure the players play to their strengths as a whole.

TEAM SELECTION

The job of selecting the strongest possible team is the major factor in the team's ultimate success or failure, and although most people feel they can pick a winning team for any match, in reality it is not quite so easy! To do this you need experience, clear thinking, judgement and often moral courage.

The coach must make a detailed and realistic assessment of his players and how he can mix and blend them effectively for the forthcoming match. He should consult with his assistant coaches as they will have been watching the players in practice sessions during the week and will be able to inform him about their mood, fitness, form, and any other information he requires. The coach and his assistants should form the tactical approach for the forthcoming match, although the responsibility for the team selection must be the decision of the coach. There must be no confusion about this – if the assistant coach does not agree with his choice of a player he should explain his reasons privately, but then abide by the coach's final decision. Remember, he will be under pressure from the supporters, directors, and the press, to select a certain player or team, but he must try to banish all this from his mind and not let emotion interfere in any way. He must keep cool and pick the team which he feels is most likely to do well in that particular match.

It will help the coach to select his players if he breaks down their individual performances into the four areas shown below.

1. **TECHNICAL**   4. **TACTICAL**   2. **PHYSICAL**   3. **PSYCHOLOGICAL**

1. Technical skill

    The coach must assess a player's techniques and skills and how reliable they are in a competitive match, since many players possess good technical ability but fail to produce it in the heat of the game. A player may possess such a strong skill that the coach decides to use the player to exploit an opponent's weakness, even though he is lacking in other areas. For example, he may bring back a player who has been out of favour for some time and who has good dribbling ability, to attack a full back who is known to be a poor defensive player. The strengths and limitations of each player's technical skill must be taken into account by the coach.

2. **Physical fitness**

Different positions and roles make different demands on fitness and the coach must be sure that the player can cope with the match requirements. For example, factors such as muddy or large pitches, hot weather, the age of the player, the fitness of opposition and role within the team will all tax the individual's level of fitness. When giving a player a certain role he must be sure that the player has the endurance to cover the ground, the strength and power to give and withstand the physical contact, and the necessary speed and agility to get away from or catch opponents. The player's physique is important in some cases; if the opposing team has a tall player who is dangerous with high crosses, then it may be necessary to select a tall player who is dominant in the air to challenge him. Coaches take calculated gambles when fielding players who are not completely fit for a one-off important match. It depends on the seriousness of the injury and whether there will be any long-term effects – if there is a danger of this, the player should not play. It should be left to the doctor and player to discuss and decide. A rigid fitness test set by the club trainer will help in making a decision.

3. **Psychological character**

Often coaches do not take adequate account of the personality of players when selecting the team. Selecting different personality types in a team causes different reactions – get the mixture right and you will have a positive team, since certain types of players can help each other's performance. For instance, a 'cocky', confident player can encourage a quieter player to become more assured by his positive, if sometimes risky, play; or the coach can select a particular player for a particular match where the aggression of an opponent needs to be matched or where a known nervous opponent who tends to go to pieces when beaten is there to be exploited.

Players affect and influence other players around them either positively or negatively. Often players will tolerate a player who has technical, fitness or tactical shortcomings if he can show by his personality and game that he can increase the team's morale and confidence. Players who are good competitors and thrive on physical, mental and social pressures can usually help other players to cope with physical challenge, and sometimes intimidation, and do well no matter what the stress.

This leads to one of the most important aspects of personality: the value of experience. There is no substitute for an experienced and battle-hardened player who has been through it all before. Young players often find it difficult to adapt to the unfamiliar, whether it be an over-aggressive match, a hostile crowd, a large ground, or the opposition employing a new style of play or tactic. As a result, they tend either to drop their heads and are shut out of the game or become over-excited and lose control, penalising their team by giving away free-kicks. An experienced player will keep cool, help younger players around him and generally have a calming and inspiring influence.

4. Tactical understanding

A player's ability to read the game and be in the right place at the right time, whether in attack or defence, is most valuable for the team. Players who have the soccer intelligence and game understanding to solve problems set by their opponents during the match can increase the tactical options open to the team and therefore challenge the opponents. Although the modern game increasingly requires players to be all-rounders, equally at home in defence or attack, there are always chances to use players in specialist roles, for example, asking a player to man mark a specific opponent throughout the game, or an attacker to forsake his usual free role to become a target-man who receives direct passes from the rest of the team in advanced, but limited, positions. Some players are aware of what is happening around them and have the self-discipline to react accordingly while others, although excellent technically, do not possess the tactical know-how to use their skills effectively.

The selection of players will also decide the tactical approach to the game. For example, the slow reaction of a full back can stifle the back four from pushing out to catch players offside, and this tactic cannot be employed.

The process of selecting the team

When selecting the team the coach must not be influenced by pressures from the directors, press and supporters. He must base his judgement solely on the facts. It takes a strong man to do this effectively as the coach himself may have prejudices against certain personalities, styles of play and the general way of doing things, and can let them interfere with an objective choice of player. He may have fixed ideas on how the game should be played and how players should perform and generally conduct themselves, and if they do not conform to this he is unwilling to select them, even though they are good players. For example, a player may be a quick and mobile striker, good at creating chances for others by his running, while the coach may prefer a big, strong player in a more conservative role to act as target-man. He must ignore his personal likings and friendships, loyalties and sympathies for certain players when selecting the best possible team. This will sometimes require ruthlessness since it may involve dropping a respected player, one who is a favourite with the supporters and the press, or a player who has worked hard to get back in the team after injury. If his team is beaten, he knows he will be told by many people how wrong he was!

Another problem that the coach will have to consider is whether or not to change a winning team. Some do not believe in changing, on the grounds that it would destroy the confidence and momentum built up by winning; others believe in 'horses for courses' – taking each game as it comes and selecting certain players and teams for certain matches. Sometimes coaches do not look into the total team performance objectively enough; they become too emotionally involved in a good result and blind themselves to the fact that the actual performance was moderate.

Above all, the coach must remember that no two games are the same; the art lies in selecting the best possible team for a particular match. He should consider the following when selecting the team for a competitive match.

The tactical approach

The opposition's style of play, the venue, whether the game is home or away, the type of match (for example, a league match, a cup knock-out, or a home-and-away two-legged affair), all affect the coach's thinking. Some coaches do not believe in assessing the opposition and tell their players to 'let them worry about us', in the belief that any analysis will tend to build fears in the players' minds about the strength of the opposition. I believe that even with the most experienced team some analysis of the opposition is important, so that steps can be taken to counter their strengths.

Play to your strengths

Sometimes coaches suddenly try to change the general style or system of play because of injuries or loss of form affecting key players or the team as a whole. This is fraught with danger; the team's best chance of a result is to play to their strengths and allow them to do what they are best at, whether it is to defend and counter-attack or just to attack when or where they can. The system or pattern of play which suits the talents of the available players must take precedence. For example, it is no use the coach trying to get his team to play a 4–4–2 system heavily based on defence if the team is largely made up of attacking players. The worst thing he can do is to ask his players to do something of which they are not capable; for instance, asking a creative player to do an out-and-out marking job on a dangerous opponent when he has neither the endurance nor the self-discipline to do so, or putting a player in an unfamiliar position, say a right-sided player in the left-back role where he has to control, kick and tackle, all on his weaker foot.

Many changes?

Coaches often chop and change the team when they fail to achieve success, but it is often the teams with the fewest changes who succeed, because by constantly playing together they develop better teamwork. It is the old chicken-and-egg dilemma – do the defeats cause the changes or vice-versa? Sometimes the team is doing well but luck goes against them at a few critical stages in the game; then it is only a matter of time before results start to come. The players and team have learnt a lot from the opening matches, and to change things at this stage may put them back to square one. They have overcome their teething troubles and are likely to start improving their performance. The coach can inject energy into the team by introducing a new player; however, wholesale changes may be unwise as no pattern can form and players will feel that they are not being given a fair chance. He must convince a player that he can play in a new position and that he can be coached to do so.

In 1987, whilst acting as assistant coach to the Liverpool F.C. under-20s team that played in a prestigious youth tournament in Holland, our team was grouped with one of the Eindhoven clubs (not P.S.V.), Ajax and Feyenoord. We played Eindhoven, the weakest team, in the first match and lost 0–1 after an extraordinary match during which we endured numerous goal line clearances and some 'miracle' goalkeeping, and they scored from literally their only shot of the match. The manager was angry and talked about wholesale changes when we played Ajax, one of the favourites, the following day. I reasoned with him that I still thought the 11 players he had selected for the first match were the strongest from the squad, and nothing in the game I had seen had forced me to change my mind. Luck plays its part and I felt that 99 times out of 100 we would have convincingly beaten Eindhoven. We decided to keep the same team which defeated Ajax 3–0 and went on to reach the final, losing narrowly 1–0 to P.S.V. Eindhoven.

Team competition

To perform to their maximum potential, players must be placed under a certain degree of pressure. Creating competition for places prevents complacency. When players sense that they will be in the team no matter how they perform, they become lazy. Leaving a player out of the team for a few matches can jolt him into starting work again and make him realise that he can be replaced if he does not play to his full potential. The size of the squad is important in providing competition for team places; it should not be so small that there is no adequate cover for the team in the event of loss of form, injuries or departures from the club, or so big that players cannot receive individual attention. The squad will usually consist of regulars, reserve players and a few promising youngsters, and if possible there should be sufficient players to provide competition for all positions.

Short- and long-term?

Some coaches select what they feel is the strongest team for each match, and each player is expected to perform up to standard from the start. The team is constantly changing and the players get the message: 'Deliver the goods or you're out!' This is not the way to coach; nearly all players, especially younger ones, require a settling-in period during which they will make mistakes as they adapt to the game at that level. The coach must show patience and tolerance with a player new to the team. Players do not develop at the same rate – some can adjust quickly, some burst on to the scene and fade away, while others adapt and improve gradually after a number of competitive matches. Coaches must seek consistency from their players, but must accept that they will not always get it, especially with young players who are still developing.

Some players show great potential but will only fulfil this with match experience, physical and emotional maturity, and careful handling – a lot depends on how the team is doing at the time. If the team is heading for promotion or relegation, the coach will usually play safe by using his regular, experienced players. However, if the team is in a position where there is not much at stake, he can experiment for the future by 'blooding' newcomers to the team or switching others around to play in a new role.

Timing selection

The best time to select the team is at least two days before a match but after the final serious training/coaching session, thus ensuring that the training effort is kept to a maximum for as long as possible but that players do not lose valuable nervous energy wondering whether or not they will be playing. For maximum effect the coach should pick the best psychological moment to inform the squad of his selection. For example, before the England v West Germany World Cup Final in England in 1966, when there was much speculation in the media about who would play – newcomer Geoff Hurst of West Ham United, or Jimmy Greaves, the experienced Tottenham Hotspur striker – the then England team manager Alf Ramsey secretly informed Hurst that he had been selected, thus alleviating his anxiety. Players should be the first to know the team selection and should certainly know before the press.

When I was youth manager at Liverpool in the mid-1980s, Kenny Dalglish, the team manager, introduced the idea of only naming his team to the press at the last possible moment, a totally different approach to what had gone before at Anfield. For decades, Bill Shankly had named his team confidently to the world two days before the match, and his successors, Bob Paisley and Joe Fagan, had seen no reason to alter this time-honoured ritual. Dalglish won the double of League and F.A. Cup in his first season so for that period the new concept seemed to work.

There could be certain advantages in naming your team at the last minute, such as not giving the opposition time to know how you intend to play, keeping your own players on their toes and keeping your options open to any late changes. On the other hand, it could cause excess tension for the players waiting to know if they have been selected, it leaves you no time to prepare your tactics as a team or may even cause a lack of confidence in some players. The coach must think carefully about when to announce his team selection.

Dropping a player

The coach often has to make unpopular and unpleasant decisions which result in players being dropped from the team to make way for others. The way this is done is very important, as the manager can end up either with a partially placated player who accepts that his form has not been good, or with an angry player who feels that he is being made the scapegoat for the team's lack of success. A coach may drop a player for a variety of reasons, such as loss of form, tactical reasons, injury or lack of match experience. He will need courage and tact to do this, as the player in question may be the type who always gives one hundred per cent effort. To build his team effectively the coach may have to experiment a little with his squad, which means that he will need to drop players temporarily who may end up becoming eventual regulars in his team. To avoid conflict he must be as sensitive as possible so that it does not negatively affect his team building plans.

When and how to drop a player

A major problem for the coach is deciding when to drop a player. To drop a player after one bad game is to admit bad judgement in selecting him in the first place. Does one poor performance mean the chop or should the player be given further chances to show what he can do? The coach must be objective and pin-point exactly why the player produced a poor performance. It could be for a variety of reasons, such as team-mates performing poorly and thus affecting his own play, an early mistake which destroyed his confidence, illness or a slight injury. Players are more likely to be resentful and angry if they are dropped without warning or if they feel the decision to be unfair in some way.

In general, players are not dropped because of one poor game; usually they are going through a period of indifferent form. The coach must then tell the player that his form is inadequate and that he must show improvement in certain areas of his game, so that when a player is dropped he has at least had some indication of why. Whenever possible, he should let the player know before anyone else that he has been dropped, since to hear the news from a team-mate, a newspaper, or another source can only be bad for his confidence. By informing the player discreetly that he is being left out for the forthcoming match, the coach

103

allows the player himself to tell his team-mates or others; this is better for his self-respect.

The best time to inform players will depend on a number of factors, such as the need to select the team in order to begin coaching for a forthcoming match, or whether he has his full complement of players or is waiting for fitness reports on others later in the week. I find that there is some artificiality in always letting a player know he is being dropped before anyone else, both for the player and the coach. The player senses what is coming as you approach him, say on the Thursday before a Saturday match, as you have already had to do it two or three times previously during the season. There has to be an acceptance by all of the best way to do what is needed for the good of the team.

Motivating players to get back in the team

Players will differ in their reactions to being dropped – some will get angry, some depressed and some will accept the situation and fight hard to get back in the team. The coach must treat each individual accordingly and must support them without allowing self-pity or unrealistic excuses. Ideally, the player should feel concern for the team. Reports on his second team matches should be studied closely by the first team coach, and his attitude to training should also be assessed. He should inform the player that if he does his job on the pitch, he cannot be kept out of the team – it is up to the player to re-build his confidence and game. Sometimes a coach will drop a player who has become complacent and feels that his position is assured no matter what happens – the sudden jolt of being dropped from the team, especially if it does well without him, may push him to better performances. This should not be done too often, and careful thought must be given to the likely consequences.

THE SUBSTITUTE

Soccer is learning to come to terms with the use of the substitute. Players feel they are failures when substituted during a competitive match, and there have been several unpleasant incidents involving players who were substituted. These incidents detract from the image of all concerned. The coach needs to convince the fans, his staff and in particular the players in his care, that the substitute can be a tactical advantage to the team and is an integral part of the game. He must make sure that all players realise the importance of the substitute. To follow are some guidelines for the coach to consider when using the substitute.

Education

Before the season begins, the coach should talk to the players about the use of a substitute during matches. This talk can be communicated to the fans via newspapers, radio or television, and an explanation given of why substitutions are made – to support players. This idea must be repeated over and over again so that players gradually accept the need to use the substitute sensibly for the team's benefit.

Procedure

The coach should work out a set procedure for substitutions, which is sensitive and effective, and saves the player's face wherever possible. The player should be warned during a lull in play a few minutes before he is due to come off to prepare him for his withdrawal. The idea of holding up a number to indicate which player is to come off is a good one, but it should be done quickly and without fuss. It helps if the trainer meets the player as he leaves the field and goes to the dressing room for treatment for injuries. If he is not injured, the trainer should make sure the player puts on his tracksuit for warmth and comfort and joins him in the trainer's box.

Integration

The substitute must feel he is a part of the team. This can be done by making sure he is involved in the full warm-up with the other players and that he understands his likely role in the game. He must be warm and ready for action and the club should provide him with a good tracksuit in cold weather.

Motivation

Players can be substituted for a variety of reasons, for example, an injury that slowed a player down, a loss of form and confidence, or a tactical switch to cover a weakness or to exploit a situation. The substitute can be used to stimulate the team by warming up vigorously on the side-line so that the players feel their position is threatened and consequently put in increased effort. In my opinion, this tactic has only limited use and may make the substitute feel that he is being used. The coach must also think about what type of player he selects as a substitute for any one game. Sometimes he might 'blood' a promising youngster in the last 20 minutes of a home match, or he might substitute a good defensive player to defend a slender lead away from home or an attacking player in extra-time at home to try to win the game.

The coach must decide if and when to use the substitute, since if he is introduced fairly early in the game and an injury occurs the team has limited options. He must also decide if a change of personnel will upset the team system and rhythm or be a boost to a flagging team. While I was a coach at Liverpool F.C. I noticed that on occasions the substitutes were telling the coach to get them on the field, so motivated were they to play!

As the coach begins to build his team he therefore needs to be aware of the part his substitutes can play over the season and how he can fully maximise their potential.

THE TEAM CAPTAIN

A good relationship between the coach and the team captain, and between the players and the team captain is important to success.

Captains vary in their personalities and approach to the job, but whatever they are like, to be effective they must get the best out of the other players. Basically, the coach should select someone who has similar ideas to his own, and try to see that his plans are carried out during the game. The coach must identify a potential captain as soon as possible and give him some responsibility with groups of players to see how he reacts to the different players and how the players react to him. Players can be groomed for captaincy by the coach over a fairly long period, so that when the time comes for them to take over the team they will be well prepared for the job. Many great teams had team managers and captains who worked closely together with their coach to achieve success, for example Sir Alf Ramsey and Bobby Moore (England), Helmut Schon and Franz Beckenbauer (West Germany), Carlos Menotti and Daniel Passarella (Argentina).

The coach must make the captain's responsibilities clear at the outset to prevent any misunderstandings. For example, if the captain changes a player from one position to another during the game and the coach does not approve, conflict may arise. After the coach and captain have agreed on the limits of his responsibility, the coach must support any decisions made by the captain.

The choice of team captain must fall on a player who is liked and respected by the majority of the team. Some captains can motivate their teams by verbal exhortation and drive, while others work by quiet example. The coach must make time to train and prepare the aspiring 'skipper' for the job, for many potential troubles can be spotted before they occur by having experience of similar situations. The team manager can train the coach by discussion and by allowing him experience in handling players.

Just like the team manager, the team captain needs personal qualities to succeed. The following are vital ingredients.

Leadership

The team captain must want to take responsibility and want to lead others by his example. He must be determined and have a strong motivation to win, which he can transmit to other players. Players tend to work for a leader who can operate effectively in competitive circumstances, where the psychological pressure is high and courage and a clear head are required.

Maturity

The team captain must gain the other players' respect by his personality. To do this, he must be consistent in temperament, assess each situation coolly, and have the necessary concentration and power of command to guide the players. He must be able to keep himself in check emotionally and must control the team by knowing all his players and how they are likely to react under pressure. The captain need not be the best performer in the team, but he should be consistent because he will find it hard to lead and persuade others to play well if he is not doing so himself. Communication between the team captain and the players must be excellent. Sometimes a youngish player can make a good captain if he has the maturity; however experience normally counts when selecting your captain.

Inspiration

The team captain, through his approach and example, must be able to inspire his players often – during practice sessions as well as during matches. He must be able to inspire the nervous player and subdue the over-confident player. So, what is the ideal position for the team captain?

Players like the team captain to be near them on the field of play if possible, to give them support. Some positions are too far from the centre of activity to be effective (e.g. winger, goalkeeper). Midfield is often considered a good position, but the average player will not have the time to see what is happening or to help others. Central defenders are usually in a good position physically to see the entire field of play and still be in relatively close contact with other positions. They will also have more time to assess play and be able to pass on information.

Summary

The coach's relationship with the team captain is important as it assists the solidarity and unity of the team. However, one thing is of paramount importance – the captain must be a good player himself who can perform consistently: if he can't he will be dropped by the manager like any other player. Good captains do not exist in large quantities so the coach needs to spot, encourage and develop one from within his squad.

CHAPTER 6
MOTIVATING THE TEAM

The coach can have a considerable motivational effect on his team, depending on his personality and his understanding of how players feel and react, and on the methods he uses. Too many coaches treat players as if their brains were separate from the rest of their body; such coaches know little about how motivation affects players. They think that getting 'psyched up' will affect players in their team in the same way, which is not often the case. It is relatively easy to get players wound up for a match; it is another thing to motivate them to such a degree that their confidence, aggression and enthusiasm are at its maximum for each individual.

Players may not be psyched up correctly for the match and as a result will perform badly. Almost all players have the potential to respond easily to crude forms of motivation, especially when they are anxious about the outcome of a forthcoming match. In these cases it is relatively easy to encourage players to become over-aggressive. Many clubs have suffered from the 'fix bayonets and charge' motivator, who looks upon a game as a battle and nothing else. The coach must teach players to come to terms with their psychological weaknesses and strengths as well as their technical, tactical and physical ones in order to control them effectively. The personal motives of the coach are important in that only by understanding his own motivations can he understand the effect they will have on his players. The coach must ask himself – and answer honestly – the following questions.

- What do I want from my players and the game?
- What are my principles and standards of sportsmanship?
- How important is winning and losing? How far will I go to attain this?
- How do I expect the game to be played?

All motivation is personal, and many players lack consistency of performance for a variety of reasons which may include low confidence, over-aggressiveness, timidity, anxiety, lack of concentration, or fear. These mental blocks prevent a player from performing at his peak. To overcome them the coach must find out what causes these blocks and seek to remove them so that the player can fulfil his potential. He can watch a player go through the motions in a morning training session, or observe him in a club practice match and be completely unimpressed. The same evening, before the crowd and in the competitive match, he looks like a world beater – the first two routines had failed to motivate him but the evening match did. The almost universal belief that professional soccer players are highly motivated because of high financial rewards is not necessarily true. The basic drives towards improvement in the game were established when they were youngsters, long before the earnings' incentive was apparent. All players have the capacity to improve psychologically, but, as with skills, fitness and tactics, it also requires patience, sensitivity and understanding. The coach who uses his players to boost his own ego by satisfying unfulfilled ambitions, or by trying to work out his own character flaws through them, is thoroughly misguided and will surely run into trouble.

When considering motivation the coach must accept that all players are different, and although most will respond well to conventional methods of motivation, others will require a different approach.

PRINCIPLES OF MOTIVATION

Player involvement

The coach will get more from his players, and increase their confidence and understanding of the game, by involving them in everything he does where possible. He should explain not only what to do but why they are doing it, so that the players are involved mentally and physically in such things as team talks and offering individual opinions on how to overcome problems. The players should be responsible for their game and motivation should be internal. Giving ownership of the team in some shape or form back to the team will increase the desire to improve.

Balanced training programme

Nothing demotivates players more than a training session that is disorganised and lacks balance of content. The programme should be well planned and should cater for the individual's and the team's needs by giving players opportunities for success during the session and also ensuring that they have a sufficient variety of activities to keep them involved. Generally, players who are highly motivated and want to improve do not need as much variety as players who are not so motivated and cannot, or will not, concentrate on what the coach is doing for long periods. This type of player needs a change of activity fairly often in order to maintain his interest. The key motivator in soccer practice is the ball!

Setting objectives

The coach must, whenever possible, give his players something to aim for and motivate them to greater efforts. He must get to know each of his players well, for without knowing their fears, ambitions, etc., it will not be possible for him to set effective objectives for them. Short- and long-range targets should be set with suitable rewards if the targets are met. Objectives that are worth the effort of the players and which will benefit their play in some way should be set. He should design these so that the player or the team experiences early success, but gradually the objectives should get more difficult to achieve so that the players are contin-ually being stretched. Objectives can be set for players to score a certain number of goals per month or season, make a number of first-team appearances as a 'newcomer' to the squad, or for the team to amass so many points within a certain time or to get more possession of the ball in their matches. Competition against himself or against team-mates within the training programme, if used properly, can help a player to improve and reach his objectives. Incentives are most important to the players and must be used carefully by the coach. He must find out what incentives motivate which players most, e.g. pride in one's performance, doing better than others, financial or material incentives, or more esteem among team-mates. The incentives must be commensurate with the importance of the objectives set, and should not appear trivial to the players. The coach, in conjunction with the players, should regularly evaluate and reset the objectives.

Training atmosphere

Wherever possible, the coach must try to create an attractive learning and practice environment for his players. The atmosphere around the training area should be as free from noise and distractions as possible to allow players to concentrate. The area should be attractive in terms of a flat, grassy and marked areas and a bright dressing room, as there is nothing worse for a coach and his players than a dark, cold, wet and depressing training area which will dampen everyone's spirits. All equipment should be laid out so that it has a visual impact for the players. The general training atmosphere will be affected greatly by the current individual and team form. If the team is on a losing run the training atmosphere should be vibrant and as free from stress as possible to help motivation and to accelerate learning.

The coach's personality

All the above mentioned principles of motivation are of secondary importance to the coach and how he organises matters. He can make a drab dressing room come alive and can also make the training field an enjoyable place on which to practise. His manner will be his own; however, he must be positive, relaxed and firm when necessary and be able to lift his players when needed. He should set examples of appearance, conduct and punctuality to his players and earn their respect. He should also get to know his players by talking to them, where possible at each session, even if it is only a few words to build up the trust and respect of his players. Nearly all players have known coaches for whom they would run through brick walls! This respect is not due to him because of his position – it has to be earned over a long period.

The coach should be an enthusiastic and inspiring leader, and the players will follow his example if they respect him. There will be a severe loss of confidence if they are losing regularly, and this is where he must be at his best and work hard to persuade players to 'get their heads up'. He must show courage by identifying himself with his players, to demonstrate that he supports them and shares in their defeat. It is only human to dissociate yourself from a losing team, but nothing could be worse – for the players or the coach. They must not blame bad luck, wallow in self-pity, or become angry or depressed; instead they must all accept responsibility, find out what is going wrong and put it right. There are few problems for the coach when the team is winning – everyone wants to play and train. However, he must be aware of complacency when all is going well; he must remember that things will not always be so good! He should be wary of this and keep one step ahead by pushing the players and maintaining the momentum.

Guidelines
Emphasise strengths
Too many coaches are negative and continually look for flaws in their players – this often de-motivates them. Look for strengths and tell players that you believe in them and their skills. Be sincere, a coach will lose credibility if he tells a player he is good at something when he knows he is not. A player is more receptive to working on his weaknesses when you have first mentioned his strengths.

Motivation in training
The basic problem for the coach is how to make a period of physical and mental stress an interesting and productive experience for the players. The players should come to the session with some eagerness and should not treat it as a necessary chore. He can assess the effect of his coaching programme by the manner in which the players approach the session. If they are lifeless and apathetic, the coach will have problems and will need to re-assess his programme. His dream is for the players to come to the practice session full of zest and enthusiasm to learn – this can be achieved by a carefully-planned motivational programme, with the coach present at each practice session, but it is not easy to attain.

Training targets
Players love competition and also like to know how they are doing in a session. The coach can record scores and achievements on charts or record cards, showing things such as times and number of runs, number of points, etc., for different groups. The pre-season period is especially good for this; however, goal setting should be done for all individual players with targets for both matches and training sessions.

Quality of programme

The coach must provide a balanced programme which is not only physically taxing, but also mentally stimulating for players. The methods, practices, drills, rhythm and continuity of the programme should ideally maintain motivation.

Change of face

No matter how well motivated, the players will become bored with the same face day after day. It is a good idea to change the club's coaches around occasionally so that they work with a new squad, or, better still, bring in a specialist to work with the players on a permanent or temporary basis. For example, clubs have been known to introduce athletic coaches, aerobic dance teachers, goalkeeping coaches, movement trainers, etc., with success. Care must be taken, however, that the specialists do not depart from the general programme, or cause injuries.

SUSTAINING MOTIVATION

The coach must provide sound leadership, which transmits itself through the team captain to the squad of players, and sustain motivation over the playing season. Coaches vary in their personalities and their style of motivation; for example, some have a dynamic style while others have a quieter, more thoughtful approach. I am made constantly aware of the way coaches and team captains go about getting the job done, often with the same results whatever the approach. Sustaining motivation throughout the season is one of the most difficult tasks for a coach since the team's moods, cohesion and attitudes will shift as their form and match results fluctuate. He must use his common sense, personality and all available staff and resources in a practical way to build up different individuals into a closely-knit group who help each other and overcome any problems they meet. This will not be easy and will greatly tax his patience, energy and perseverance, especially if things start to go wrong with individuals or the team; this is where he will have to show his ingenuity. The coach, team captain and players need to work with, not against, each other to achieve success; to be effective over a season the team needs co-operation, drive and continuous motivation.

The coach

He must want his team and himself to do well in the game. A 'never-say-die' attitude that gets through to his players can make them develop the same feeling and thus get the best performance out of them. If he does not believe in himself it is going to very difficult for him to motivate his team.

The team captain

He must have a willing mentality. He must have respect for the other players and for the captain. If he has the personality to influence the players on and off the field, then the team has a psychological advantage.

The players

The players must want to be winners and must be prepared to endure set-backs such as injuries, defeats and loss of form to gain eventual success.

Teams such as Liverpool, Manchester United, Arsenal, AC Milan, Real Madrid and Ajax have all had psychologically superior teams over the past few decades, due to highly motivated staff and players all working towards the same objective.

Individual players' and the team's form ebbs and flows throughout the season. The team will be playing one or two matches a week and will be trying to reach the peak of physical and mental performance for each match over a number of matches and over a long period of time. It is hard for players to maintain enthusiasm, maximum effort and motivation towards practices and matches during this extended period. The coach must make sure that this does not become a problem.

Many coaches like to see their team go to the top early in the season as 'front-runners', while others are happier if their team is lying within striking distance of the leaders and where the pressure on them is not so great.

League position

The position of the team in the league at any time is important, as it will guide the coach on how he motivates the team. There are three categories: high in the table – on top or near the top and possible league winners; mid-table – around half-way, i.e. relatively safe from relegation but too far away from promotion; near the bottom – on or near the bottom with relegation a distinct possibility.

1. **High in the table**

    The coach's job is to maintain the momentum by giving the players increased coaching and fitness work. However, he must look out for over-confidence and complacency in his players, and when he spots it he must be prepared to give players a jolt to get them concentrating again. On the other hand, players may start to show signs of mental and physical staleness, which may be caused by pressure from being at the top of the league or by fatigue. In such an instance the player can be rested for a week or so away from the soccer environment, or the training programme can be varied to include less fitness work. Both of these approaches may improve the player's well being and zest for the game.

2. **Mid-table**

This position is often the coach's biggest motivational problem, as the team will have no real incentives such as promotion or relegation to fight for or against. The players still want to win, but often they will find it difficult to build themselves up for the match, and this feeling can be transmitted to or from the coach, thus decreasing the motivation. Often, teams below them will beat them because they are more highly motivated, while they in turn will often win against teams above them for the same reason. The team shows occasional flashes of what it is capable of, but the sense of urgency is gone and the team begins to stagnate. The coach must re-motivate himself and put new objectives before his players, possibly preparing for the next season by buying in new players, or experimenting by placing players in different positions, or by developing new systems of play.

3. **Near the bottom**

Teams in this position will usually begin to develop a defeatist and negative attitude in their play, which in effect means a loss of confidence. The players may go through the motions of declaring that they will win the next match, but inwardly they may believe that they will be beaten and, as a consequence, they play erratically from fear, afraid to take chances. Through his attitude and personal example of calmness and patience with the players and their problems, the coach must remove the fear element from the situation. He must not become over emotional with players, thus increasing the pressure on them, instead, he must support them and assure them that if they keep doing the things they are good at the situation will improve.

The coach must stop the players from thinking about the results, and instead start them thinking about reaching the individual objectives that he has set them, simplifying each individual's role in the team and giving him a target for which to aim in the match. For example, 'Mark a certain player from the other team', 'Hit early crosses into the goal area', or 'Shoot at every available chance'. At half time and after the match, the coach should focus the players' attention on the things he gave them to do, praise them when they did well and encourage the others who may have been struggling. This will give them something to build on.

Before the match

The coach must try to get the correct level of emotional tension in each individual and in the team as a whole for maximum performance in the match. This is difficult to do, as he can over-excite players or fail to see that they require stimulus, both of which will mean an erratic performance. He will attempt to motivate his team in a variety of ways – emotional excitement, reason and conditioning – to get players to focus in specific ways on their own and their opponents' game in order to beat them. Individuals vary in their pre-game preparation and the process of 'getting set' starts as soon as the players begin to think about the forthcoming match, which may be weeks, days or even hours before kick-off.

When getting his team ready to meet a certain team in a match, the coach prepares them on the basis that they will play a team that is more successful, less successful or on a par with themselves. The preparation for each of these categories could be different. The following points should be considered.

1. **Playing a more successful team**

   When meeting a team like this, it is often a good idea to give the players a feeling of being the 'underdog' which may lend them a psychological advantage. However, if they feel that, due to the opponents' reputation, they have no chance then the coach must go to work to make the team see that the opposition has certain weaknesses, which can be exploited.

2. **Playing an equally successful team**

   The coach must try to gain a psychological advantage for his team by challenging his players to show that they are better without any doubt. Whichever way he can, he must gain an advantage for his team. Past results can be used to show how the games were won or lost.

3. **Playing a less successful team**

There is a danger of over-confidence here that the coach must put right. Often, no matter how the coaches try to make the players see the seriousness of the situation, the players, although they may seem to be preparing properly, do not train during the week with the same urgency and as a result perform badly. The players seem subconsciously to relax, thinking that they will win the game without moving into top gear, and as a consequence they are not motivated enough for the game. When they do start to realise that they have a fight on their hands, they often find that they cannot raise their motivational level sufficiently to retrieve the game. When playing teams who are near to relegation, it is easy for the players to become complacent. This sort of thing does happen and players must understand why.

FINDING THE RIGHT MOTIVATIONAL LEVEL

The degree of motivation and stimulation of a player is vital. If it is too near either end of the scale, the player's performance can be disrupted. The job of finding the correct mind-set for his players is a difficult one for the coach. Players may be too high or too low for a variety of reasons, only some of which may be discovered by the coach. Factors such as confidence in his own team's ability and the closeness and importance of the forthcoming match, can all influence the player's level of motivation for the fixture. The problem for him is not merely to get the player geared up for the match, but to raise or lower him to the correct level of excitement. The coach must watch for signs of a player's attitude pre-match and take decisive action if he feels the player is displaying negativity.

Signs to look for

The first physical signs that a player is getting ready for action is when the heart and lung rates begin to increase and the muscle groups start to tense. Individuals can exhibit signs such as shaking or trembling of limbs, excessive sweating, frequent trips to the toilet, ceasing to talk or talking more than usual, stomach cramp or vomiting (a few top-class players are sick fairly regularly before a match). It will be obvious that players who are inexperienced and who do not have the necessary skills, fitness and tactical understanding ingrained in their systems will be disrupted by nervousness. For example, skills which demand fine muscular touch and rapid decisions will be very difficult, if not impossible, to produce in a competitive match. The coach must also remember that motivation and excitement are contagious and that a player or team can be affected by others or by the situation. A team that is under-motivated before a match can sometimes be aroused by a comment made by the opposition's coach, for example that his team will annihilate their team. It must be remembered, however, that the over-excitable coach is a liability and if he cannot control his emotions he may push his team over the top psychologically.

Guidelines

Play up or play down the importance of the match

Over-excited players can often be calmed down by placing the match in its proper perspective – it's not World War III. It's very important but it's still only a game. The reverse procedure can be used with the player who is apathetic and does not seem to be very interested in playing. The coach can stress the importance of the match, the size of the crowd and the financial incentives, or mention whatever is likely to motivate the player. In this way he can play up or down the importance of the match and help to regulate the players motivation to the correct level.

Accepting responsibility

The coach can take pressure off a player who is too keyed-up by speaking to him and reassuring him that provided the player tries to follow the pre-match plans set out by him, he has no need to worry as the coach will accept the responsibility for failure. Equally, players who are too low must be made to accept responsibility for their contribution to the outcome – and the post-mortem to come later!

Dressing room atmosphere

The presence of others in the dressing room can have a disruptive effect, so only the coach and the team which is playing should be present. Reserve players should be sent out and the door closed so that the coach and players can prepare effectively. Individual clubs sometimes believe in keeping the squad together as a 'family' to prepare in a ritual way for the match, while others feel that match preparation is an individual thing and that players should get rid of any excess nervous tension in their own way. Some may sit quietly, while others may involve themselves in horseplay – which should be stopped if taken to extremes. As a rule, the coach, by his own example, should continually educate his players to prepare properly and remind the players that they can let their hair down after they have won, not before!

The coach's pep talk

The coach can affect players' motivational levels by a properly conducted pep talk. He should understand that each player is different and a simple, direct appeal by him to the team is likely to affect the players to a lesser or greater degree. Sometimes, he can bring in his assistant who may be better at motivating a certain player or calming the players down when they are too tense. The coaches can operate in this way, using their different personalities to help regulate the motivation level of the players.

Pre-game warm up

The warm up can be designed specifically to raise or lower the team's motivation levels. Players who are too tense can reduce their anxiety and tension level by the use of a good pre-game warm up which will 'fire' them slightly and as a result relax them. It is important physically and psychologically in preparing the players for battle, and the duration and intensity will depend on the players' needs and the particular situation. Often, players will 'drop' or get too 'high' just before a match, due to travel problems or anxiety about the outcome of the game, and this can leave them feeling weak, tired and sickly. The warm-up can be useful for releasing excess tension or cheering up a player in these circumstances. It can also help to alleviate players' fears before a game by getting them gradually accustomed to the playing area, crowd and atmosphere, and giving them the chance to rehearse their techniques and skills. Most professional clubs have devised a sound warm-up routine, while some individual players have their own specific routine to prepare them for the match.

Psychological pressure

Players are prey to doubts and fears that put them under pressure before the match and which, as a result, inhibit their performance (e.g. fear of physical intimidation and injury, fear of facing a certain player, etc.). If the player is not confident of his own team's ability to do well against the opposition, he will have anxieties, which in turn will undermine his chances of success. The coach must be careful in selecting a new player for a competitive match, as putting a young and inexperienced player into the team too soon, with the result that he performs badly, can have a very damaging effect on his confidence and he will find it difficult to recover from his experience. It takes a certain type of personality within a young player to cope with the psychological pressures of increased tempo and a more physical approach in the game, and hostility from the fans. The coach is responsible for preparing his players for competition and knowing when they are ready, not only in the skills, tactical and fitness sense, but also psychologically. As soon as he thinks that a player is ready for inclusion in the team, he should prepare him gradually by increasing pressure (similar to that in the real match) until he can learn to control his emotions. Some players need longer to prepare than others. The coach must be patient and adapt his approach to the player's needs, making sure that he does not lose patience and rush things. The following guidelines will help the coach prepare his player psychologically for a match.

Get to know your player

The coach must get to know the player as quickly as possible and try to diagnose why the player is anxious or weak in certain areas. If the player is receptive and open with him in informal discussions, he might be able to discover what some of his problems are. One of the most vital skills that the coach can have is his ability to gain his players' trust and get to know the player as a human being. Coaches who have this knack are in a position to help the player in a variety of ways.

Obtain help from other sources

Often it is difficult to get through to a player who for some reason is over-anxious and protective. Discreet enquiries can be made which might give the coach an insight into any possible problems. The coach, however, must be sensitive and ethical in obtaining this information, because should the player think the coach has been going behind his back he will cease to respect him. The information can be acquired in casual conversation and often it can be most useful in helping the coach to find out what the problem might be and how best to solve it.

Look for signs

Players who are over-tense can show signs of anger when confronted with psychological pressure, especially those with limited self-control. Some players lose confidence and do not try to perform their skills in the game. They become quiet and isolated from team-mates. In others, defence mechanisms take over, and the player will blame everyone except himself for his errors; or a player may become so anxious about his performance in the match that he is angry with himself or aggressive with coach and team-mates. Knowing the player is doing these things will help the coach to realise that the player needs help in coming to terms with the pressure of the game. Coaches need to learn how to read their players' body language because this skill will give them much valuable information.

Therapy

A player's tensions can be lowered by the careful use of hot and cold baths or showers, massage, the playing of relaxing music, or heated rooms with beds to lie on.

When the coach thinks that he has identified a problem, he must find the best way of lessening or removing the circumstances that affect the player so that he can withstand and live with the psychological pressure of the match. The coach can perhaps help by designing the practice session near to the level of stress that will be encountered in the match and by conditioning players to perform their skills and play the game well when under pressure.

Superstition

Many players have relatively harmless superstitions, such as coming out of the dressing room last, touching a certain boot, or holding a ball. Why do they do this? Basically, they are anxious about the forthcoming match, and anxiety breeds superstition. How should the coach treat superstition? If the players have little rituals that do not appear to interfere with their performance, they should be tolerated. However, if a player is constantly changing his superstitions and blaming things such as bad luck, 'jinx teams', or something he did differently that day, the coach must get the player to accept responsibility for his own performance. He must show by his own attitude that the team should not rely on luck to win matches, but should instead focus on the real factors that either win or lose matches. If they lose, players must accept that certain things went wrong – not events outside their control, but errors that can be put right!

A considerable number of players allow their minds to be set for the remainder of the game by the outcome of the first touch of the ball, believing that accurate passes equal good performances and vice versa. For example, some players will give an easy first pass, an aggressive player may make sure that he stops his opposite number with the first tackle to intimidate him, or a team may channel the ball back through the team for the goalkeeper to get a touch of it in comfortable circumstances. By his own positive attitude, the coach can help the players to realise that this is unreasonable and that making a mistake in the first minute is the same as making a mistake in the last. The warm-up should provide players with plenty of opportunities to touch the ball, thus allowing them to experience early success or make their mistakes before the game!

Summary

Motivation is one of the coach's key factors in gaining success, and it will greatly depend on his personality, attitude and methods of getting players interested in becoming better performers and accepting the means by which they can develop. His understanding of team dynamics and how different personalities interact together will be essential. He must never miss an opportunity to learn from wherever he can get the art and signs of motivating the team.

CHAPTER 7
DEVELOPING TEAMWORK

Successful teams exhibit great teamwork. All coaches try to achieve maximum co-operation between individuals but are often disappointed by a player's or team's response. Building-up and maintaining teamwork is a very difficult task for the coach as players differ in their degree of responsibility to the team. Some are selfish, only wanting to do things that make them look good while other exhibit inconsistent behaviour that causes irritation to their team-mates.

The team's level of success will rise and fall throughout the season and at some time the team will hit a losing streak, with injuries and problems within the club. This tests the loyalties, patience and responsibility of coach and players to the limit, and this is where teamwork is most important. In situations like this it is easy to blame something or someone else for individual failure and the coach must realise that there can be hidden disharmony in the team. For example, there is likely to be rivalry between two or more players for positions in the team, personality clashes between the coach or players, and jealousy of the so-called star player in the team. The problem for him is to get the players working with, not against, each other, for as long as it takes for success to come.

The coach must consider the following factors when trying to build up teamwork at the club.

THE COACH'S ATTITUDE

The coach and his assistants all have a profound effect on teamwork at the club. He must accept full responsibility for the team image and conduct, whether positive or negative. A team which consistently involves itself in foul and vicious play, or has unsporting attitudes, probably has a coach who does not have the strength of character to control the players, turns a blind eye to their conduct as long as they keep winning, or may even encourage violent play as a team policy. One would hope to change the thinking of such a coach if at all possible, but if not, they must be stood up to in the hope that they will be forced out of the game.

The coach must have the moral courage to stand up for his principles, and take full responsibility for his team's image and conduct. The staff must work to develop respect from players and also encourage respect between players. This is not easy, as it will involve players and staff showing tolerance of aspects of human behaviour that they may not like, but it is important; players who do not get on well socially are likely to carry their resentments on to the field of play and team spirit suffers as a consequence. It is unrealistic to expect all players to adjust to each other's personalities and behaviour in the same way; however, serious team problems can be minimised by the staff team. All staff must co-operate to help problem players re-adjust to the team. The coach can gain the help of the other players in being tolerant of a player's excesses of behaviour by pointing out to them that the player can become an asset to the team.

Teamwork can also be developed by organising tours or similar events where the players are brought together, and new friendships can be formed. The coach can arrange small competitions or events where players need to work together to win. It has been known for squads of players at several clubs to go on survival courses in winter, where they went on bleak moors in snow and freezing temperatures with only a tent to protect them from the elements, and with very little food. The idea of such courses is to develop a sense of comradeship and teamwork in adverse conditions in the hope that this will carry through to the competitive match.

THE TEAM CAPTAIN

The team captain can do much to influence teamwork and for this reason it is important to select a player who is a natural leader. During the season, various potential team captains will emerge – for example, the player who leads by personal example, the one who inspires by his verbal exhortations and presence, or the one who is the general or playmaker and who dictates the game by directing and persuading the other players. The team captain has responsibilities off the field as well as on it and should work in harmony with the coach to keep things running smoothly. The team captain's responsibilities will usually depend on his relationship with the coach and where the demarcation line for decision-making lies. His role is to act as the bridge between the coach and the players, assisting with the communication of information, creating teamwork, and taking responsibility for tactical changes or decisions that he deems necessary during the match. The coach needs to meet and discuss with his captain exactly what he is and is not responsible for in his role. It will obviously be of great help if they share a mutual respect and liking for the way each other works and their principles of how the game should be approached and played.

PROBLEM PLAYERS

Many players fail to realise that their success or failure depends on the team performance. Some players are selfish and cannot see beyond their own performance, while others play safe and will not take risks, which might mean that they are less than effective and do not help their team-mates when they should. There are different types of problem players who can cause disharmony in the dressing room or on the field by their complete indifference to the coach, team tactics, training and coaching programme, and club rules, and often it is the most talented individuals who cause problems by their unreasonable and uncooperative behaviour. Problem players can have a very negative effect on teamwork and the coach must be strong in identifying them and either changing their ways or allowing them to leave the club even though they are gifted.

Often problems occur when players are not selected for the first team and who feel that they are being neglected or unjustly treated. Sometimes players who have never caused problems when in the first team show a change of attitude when dropped into the reserve team. They cause disruption by lack of effort in training, by forming cliques with other players in a similar situation and spreading rumours designed to cause dissension among the other team members. The players out of

127

favour hope fervently that the first team is beaten, and I have heard a group of players from a professional league club cheer loudly when the opposition scored against their club. It is natural to feel dissatisfied and angry at being left out of the team. If players did not feel this, their motives and commitment would be in question. However, nothing is gained by wishing failure on team-mates. The only way that anyone can be guaranteed a regular first team place is by developing a positive attitude during the coaching sessions, by having confidence in the reserve team and playing so well that the coach must put the player back in the first team as soon as a suitable position arises.

The coach often needs to exercise careful judgement when deciding whether to support or condemn his players for reckless behaviour. Soccer is an emotional game and players are only human and at times can lose their cool momentarily. There is a difference in a player who normally exhibits a competitive but fare attitude to the game who has a one-off rush of blood to the head and one who is habitual offender.

TEAM TYPE

Although individuals differ in their psychological make-up, within the mix there is a team type which comes through. The two basic types are as follows.

TYPE A – COOPERATIVE	TYPE B – COMPETITIVE
This type has strong needs for friendship and co-operation among its players. Players will still get upset about losing. However, although they are disappointed they will tend to support each other through thick and thin.	This type is mainly concerned with winning and success. They are not worried about forming relationships but about functioning well as a team in order to win matches.

The coach should establish as quickly as possible which type his team tends towards and approach the players on that basis. Individuals differ in their psychological needs, such as self-esteem, being liked and respected by team-mates, and feeling part of the team. Players practise and play together regularly and although they see much of each other they may not be concerned about friendships on or off the field. As players age, they experience various situations with the team which may bring them to heights of elation with superb team performances or to the depths of despair with inept displays. As the season progresses the team spirit will change, depending on its experiences, which will tend to boost or subdue teamwork. The coach must find out where the team wants to go, how hard it is prepared to work and what price it is prepared to pay to achieve success. A balanced mix of type A and B players is important to the team's success as each type has a part to play. Many strikers need to be goal-orientated and rather selfish to score consistently, while every team needs at least one midfield player who is prepared to let others take the glory as he becomes an unsung hero working hard in the background.

POSITIVE IMAGE

The club image is important to teamwork and can affect it in a number of ways. Outsiders can see the club and team image differently from the staff and players inside the club. Teams are seen as being well organised, aggressive, skilful and athletic, or undisciplined, inconsistent and unbalanced. The image can be positive or negative, and the coach must ensure that if it is the former he builds on this to help teamwork. If it is the latter, he must work to develop a new image so that the players have confidence, belief and meaning in their part in the team, their team-mates, the coach and staff. He must see that the club image is positive and that all individual players work hard to maintain this over a long period. One serious error by a player at the wrong time can destroy or seriously damage the image.

Howard Wilkinson, during his career as coach at Leeds United F.C., decided that the glorious history of the club had paradoxically become a negative image to the team, with its past achievements almost unreachable in his day. He had a number of the old team photos and other material which reminded people of the past removed and the team enjoyed success. During the 1970/80s Wimbledon F.C. acquired a negative image for many people in the game for their intimidating tactics and play; however, this has only served to make the staff unite and work harder to beat much more glamorous opposition time and time again. What many people would view as detrimental to their image, the 'crazy gang' (as they were known at the time) accepted as being positive to their own unique image.

CHANGING THE TEAM IMAGE

If the team's image is a negative one the coach must first seek to change the players' attitudes which are often likely to affirm this image. It is much more difficult to change an individual's attitude than it is to change the team image, because it involves the individual player's emotions and beliefs which means the coach must show greater patience and determination. The interaction between him and player, and how different the desired team image is from the player's attitude, will determine what approach he should adopt with the individual player. It is important that when attempting to change the team's image, he remembers that to do this he requires the individual player's co-operation.

Develop relationships

The coach must try to have separate, informal meetings with each player so that he can get to know something about him and the things that are important to him, whether it is his wife and family, girlfriend, religion, education, ambitions or hobbies. If he is genuine in his desire to develop better relationships, the player will feel he can trust him and will be more inclined to co-operate with his plans for the team. However, if a player does not wish to discuss matters outside the game then his wishes should be respected. He must be ethical in his dealings with players and ensure that he does not break any confidences trusted to him. There is often a climate of suspicion and mistrust in the game which he must seek to remove if he wants to develop better communication, trust and ultimately teamwork.

Build up confidence

Many players lack confidence in themselves or in the team, and the coach must do everything in his power to correct this situation. He can continually praise and encourage players who are making a real effort to change their attitude, and can spend more time on the practice area and in conversation with certain players on an individual basis to support them and to make them feel more confident. Players should be encouraged to give their own opinions on what is needed to improve the team image and he should try to incorporate these in his plans where possible. A player must feel that he is a good player and the coach has a very important role to play in boosting the player's self-confidence.

Set objectives

Trouble starts at a club when the players have too much time on their hands and when they feel that the playing, training and coaching programmes are aimless.

The coach will do much to improve teamwork if he sets realistic objectives for individual players, groups and the team over the short and long term. Objectives such as fitness, skills, tactics, behaviour, number of matches played, and goals scored for and against can be set to challenge the players and team, giving them something to work towards together during the season. Goal-setting forms should be issued at the start of the season and objectives set and periodically monitored throughout. Goals should help to create a more positive team image for players.

The training programme

Players must be made to realise that training and coaching sessions are vital to the team's success and that it is the players' duty to put in the necessary practice, particularly in winter when daylight hours are short and time needs to be spent productively. The atmosphere of the practice sessions also sets the tone for the forthcoming competitive match, and poor practice can result in bad habits which will manifest themselves during the match. A new coach can help to create a new image by the way he approaches the training programme. He can change the emphasis from work with the ball to more running or vice versa. Much of the teamwork can be forged on the training ground where players are together for long periods of time.

Tactical approach

The coach can set out to change the team image by altering its tactical approach. For example, he may feel that the approach has been too limited and does not fit in with the team's strengths. He may decide to change from a playing style that has been good to look at but has not won games, to a more disciplined approach where the players do not leave themselves so vulnerable, and therefore win more matches. Alternatively he may decide that the team should become more adventurous and attack as a unit. This can have a radical effect on some teams and so needs to be carefully examined and discussed with the players and his coaches.

CHANGING THE CLUB IMAGE

The coach can create a fresh image for an old-fashioned or drab club by introducing a series of changes such as re-painting the ground, new strips, blazers or ties, new stationery, advertising slogans or club name. A logo can be designed and reproduced on letter headings, shirts, tracksuits or blazers to promote the feeling of unity and of progress. The backing of the Board, staff and players must be obtained before any changes are introduced. Everyone must believe in what they are doing for it to have full effect. The coach must communicate clearly to the players, staff and supporters, plus any other people connected with the club, what he is trying to do for the club image, through meetings, newsletters, or via the local press. Once the initial impetus has died down, he must emphasise and re-emphasise the need for the new image. This can be achieved in a variety of ways – meetings, informal discussions or reprimands for violation of the image, and also through praise when players show development and improvement in their attitude.

A CODE OF PRACTICE

To be successful, players need to be self-disciplined as individuals and as a team. For example, there are players who are always getting into trouble with referees, or who are regularly late for training sessions, or abuse their health by late nights or other excesses. A team which tends to be complacent when meeting a team lower in the league table, or which takes irresponsible risks such as defenders dribbling or inter-passing in tight situations around their own penalty area, is placing the success of the team at risk. All players differ in their levels of self-discipline and responsibility to the team; some are conscientious, some lack consistency in their behaviour, some are over-sensitive, while others do not seem to feel any concern for the team at all. Some coaches draw up a set of rules and disciplinary procedures to which each team member is subject regardless of the circumstances. I feel this is fraught with danger and could disrupt teamwork because some players will feel that they have been unjustly treated. Each player needs to be treated as an individual and each situation on its merit. To punish with a heavy fine a player who has arrived late for a training session for the first time, or to give two players an equal punishment for a similar offence, when it is one player's first offence and the other has committed several, is asking for trouble.

The type of team will determine the kind of rules and discipline that will be required to achieve success and maintain teamwork. The coach must make it clear to all players that to be effective they need to agree on a club strategy and plan which will give them the best chance of success, and that players who blatantly break the rules will be treated firmly. He must, however, realise that soccer is an emotional game where players will experience feelings of despair, depression, excitement, elation and lack of confidence. Most players, at some time or other, will go overboard in their reactions to situations. He must be careful not to over-react when this happens; players are human, and although the player may clearly have disregarded the rules and should be disciplined, the severity of the punishment should take into consideration whether or not the player has been making a determined effort to conform to the team image and code of practice. When drawing up the team rules, he must decide on the type of team that he is handling and act accordingly. For example, if the team tends to be disciplined and co-operative, there would be less need for rules, while if players were argumentative and selfish by nature, the disciplinary system would need to be stricter.

Conduct on the field of play

The players need to be clearly informed as to what is and what is not acceptable on the field of play. Some players get involved in personal vendettas with opposing players. This type of player is a liability to his team, as he cannot concentrate properly on the game. Other players often get into trouble with referees by back-chatting to them after decisions have gone against them or by losing their self-control when intimidated, physically or verbally, by opponents. Such players put themselves and the team under psychological pressure by conceding free-kicks in dangerous positions, by earning cautions or by risking dismissal. Players who constantly get into trouble require support when they are making a genuine effort to change their conduct. On the other hand it will take a continuous and firm approach to change their attitude for the better. Be a strong coach!

RELATIONSHIPS BETWEEN COACHES AND PLAYERS

There must be positive relationships between coaches and players for the team to be successful. The player must display reasonable conduct towards coaches and his team-mates, and equally coaches need to show a professional attitude towards their players. Obviously, in the competitive atmosphere of a soccer club, relationships will suffer at times. No matter how frustrated or angry players become, the coach must make each one aware of the need for respect for others. Allowances must be made by coaches for occasional arguments and outbursts, but limits for such conduct must be set, and players who overstep the mark must be fairly disciplined. The coaches need to show a united front when disputes arise; however, they should be kept within the confines of the club and not be allowed to fester where they can have a negative effect on teamwork.

Personal responsibility

The coach must make it clear that each player is responsible for his own health and level of physical fitness. Some players lack the willpower to keep themselves in shape for the competitive matches plus the many coaching and training sessions over a long season. These players must be helped by whatever means the coach has at his disposal. He should have some objective idea of each player's physical fitness and health problems, such as asthma, a suspect knee, migraines or weight gain. He should test players pre-season and during the season so that he can show the results to players who are not as fit as they ought to be and try to detect the reasons for this.

Some players' lifestyles may mean that they have inadequate sleep or an unsuitable diet; they may smoke and drink too much or not get enough relaxation. Obviously, a coach cannot dictate his players' lifestyle, but if it is interfering with playing performance, the players concerned are letting the team down and he has to take steps to rectify the situation. Some players find it difficult to keep their weight down to a reasonable level in order to be at their peak of fitness and need encouragement from the coach to do so; overweight players can have fines imposed on them. Regular fitness and health tests by the coach will help the player to discipline himself and maintain his peak condition.

The coach is solely responsible for formulating the team rules and seeing that they are kept. He should consider the following points before deciding on them.

Few rules

It is wise not to have too many rules otherwise players will begin to feel that they are being penalised for every little indiscretion. By having too many rules a coach makes things difficult for himself because it will be impossible to enforce them all. Excessive discipline will annoy players; he must use common sense when dealing with problems and formulating rules.

Fair rules

The coach must ensure that he sets fair rules which the players regard as reasonable and which are not based on his personal prejudices. The world is changing rapidly and so is soccer! Some coaches find it difficult to adjust to the changes in attitude of some younger players. Both may need to compromise to maintain effective teamwork; however, he has the responsibility and must ensure that his rules are fair for all.

Disciplinary procedure

It is usually best to deal with problems involving discipline as soon as they appear; however, occasionally a tough-minded player who is a consistent offender should be kept waiting for some time to 'sweat it out' and bring home to him the gravity of the situation. The idea of punishment is not to exact revenge for misdemeanours but rather to help the player to change his conduct for his own and the team's good, and great care is necessary when deciding on the procedure to take. For example, coaches who bring players in for extra training as a punishment after a defeat are only communicating to them that training is negative and to be avoided. There must be better ways than this to get through to players and also to maintain the team's integrity!

Clear communication

The coach should hold a pre-season meeting at which he can inform the players of the team rules and the disciplinary procedure for any infringements of the rules. To safeguard himself and the coaches, and to make sure they are known to all players, he should have details of the rules, with likely punishments where necessary, pinned to the dressing room notice-board or printed in the players' handbook. Remember though, it is always better to have discussions with the team captain and players over rules and procedure before setting them firmly in tablets of stone.

DISCIPLINARY METHODS

Players can be disciplined for such things as bad conduct on the field of play, lack of punctuality, failing to turn up for training sessions or matches without good reason, lack of effort at training sessions or foul language. The methods the coach adopts will of course depend on the severity of the offence and how it will affect teamwork. Here are some guidelines to consider.

Verbal confrontation

Often all a player requires is a firm reminder of his obligations to the team. This can be more effective in the privacy of the coach's office. Players who constantly make trouble for themselves and the team by their behaviour can **sometimes** be confronted angrily by the coach to good effect. Players who may have developed negative attitudes because they have got away with bad behaviour in the past can begin to change their attitude following a sudden jolt from the coach, who lets them know in no uncertain terms what he expects from them in the future. Verbal confrontation, however, can be fraught with danger and should be considered carefully beforehand, even by the most experienced coach.

Fines

Monetary fines can be imposed on players for lateness, misconduct on the field of play, severe arguments or squabbles with fellow players. The amount will depend on the nature of the offence. This can be quite effective providing the sums are set at the correct level; neither so excessive as to cause hardship nor so low as to be ineffectual. The idea of hitting players where it hurts is more effective in the professional or semi-professional game. Sometimes it is more acceptable to players for the money to go towards a charity or towards a break at the end of the season for the players – either way it needs to be considered carefully and discussed with the players before it is implemented.

Suspension

Players who break club rules can be suspended for a period during which they are not allowed to play in competitive matches, train with the team, or even come to the ground. The isolation of the player, especially if the team hits a winning run, can have a salutary effect on him. The length of suspension will depend on the offence. Many coaches dislike this method of discipline as it deprives them of a good player at a time when they could do with him! However, he must decide whether this method will prove to effective in the long term.

Dropping a player

As mentioned, many coaches dislike any method which deprives them of a player for a game, but in certain cases it has proved to be the necessary jolt to get players out of a complacent attitude and into a more enthusiastic frame of mind. There is a danger, however, that if a player is dropped for disciplinary reasons and the team suffers a bad result, the player may feel that the team cannot do without him, especially if he plays in the next match and the team wins. Sometimes a player or players will do something that leaves the coach with little option and if he does not take a firm approach he will lose the respect of the other players. It may have the effect of bringing home to the player how much he has let his team-mates down and as such it can maintain teamwork. This course of action should, however, be treated with caution.

DISCIPLINARY PROCEDURE

The coach must face team problems as soon and as fairly as possible, and show strength of character in dealing with them. If he ignores them or hopes that the situation will sort itself out, he is opting out of one of the most important aspects of his job.

When he decides to discipline a player he should consider the following procedure to avoid possible conflict.

The reason

He must think about why he is considering disciplinary action and he must also be clear about the possible outcome of his action. Is the offence really so severe? At times some coaches tend to over-react by confronting players when they themselves are angry. It is always a good idea for him to take some time-out and sit down to get his emotions under control before he confronts the player.

The approach

The coach must give some thought to the personality of the player and whether he is normally conscientious, excitable, or lacks responsibility. When planning his approach he should reflect on what has worked well with the player in the past. Does he normally react better to a quiet talk or to a more forceful approach? If a few methods have failed with a particular player and he has blatantly and consistently flouted the rules, the coach needs to try different approaches which may be based more on intuition than past experience, and which require close monitoring of the player's subsequent reactions to them.

The environment

Thought needs to be given to where the coach confronts the player. The training area or dressing room is most familiar to the player, while the coach's office is alien territory. He must not confront the player in front of his team-mates because the player can lose face and hold a grievance against the coach for a long time. However, it is not always possible to avoid this as sometimes the player will seek confrontation with the coach by breaking the rules in front of other players when he is present. If he is psychologically strong he can let the player know what the limits are in terms of his conduct there and then; otherwise he can try to defuse the situation by telling the player to come to his office immediately where he can confront him on his own territory. The choice of environment depends on the situation, but the office is usually more suitable for major offences; the training field, dressing rooms or the club coach are usually better for more minor matters.

Summary

There are several areas which are important to the build-up and maintenance of the teamwork, but perhaps the most influential is the coach and his assistants. He must try to make difficult players accept that their conduct is causing a problem to the team. In this way they both can work together to improve the player's attitude. At its best, teamwork is an irresistible force but to form, maintain and develop it requires determination, tact, courage, planning and patience from the coach.

CHAPTER 8
TEAM EVALUATION

In the modern game, the pressure on coaches to guide their teams to success is immense. They seek to gain advantage and increase effectiveness by out-thinking others and keeping a step ahead. One area in which they can do this is through the creation of a sound scouting and evaluation system for their club, as this can help to make decisions such as the tactics adopted by the team for the forthcoming match, whether or not to risk a transfer fee to acquire a new player, or simply to help with the running of the team. The advantages of good player or team evaluation are as follows.

REFERENCE SYSTEM

Information collected by the scouts can be systematically filed away, allowing the coach to build up a dossier of information on players and clubs for future reference. Useful information could include current details on players who may be potential signings, forthcoming opponents, or the form of some players in the existing team. Many top clubs have a sophisticated computerised information system of players worldwide.

Tactical dossiers

The team can get access to detailed information about the opposition which can prepare them for their style of play. Strengths and weaknesses can be detected which can be exploited or given special attention in the game-plan. It can also be useful for the coach in acquiring details about his own team which can allow him to change his coaching practice to combat weaknesses in the teams play.

Confidence

Knowing that the coach has done his usual meticulous job in analysing the opposition will help the players to feel more secure and confident about the forthcoming match. There is nothing worse than going into a fierce competitive match away from home knowing little about the opponents, the ground, the playing field, the crowd, the system of play or other such factors.

The same principle applies when trying to sign new players for the club. The more information you have about the player, the more impressed he is likely to be with the club, and the greater the possibility of a successful conclusion in the quest to sign him.

Realistic practice

Advance knowledge of the opposing team's strengths, weaknesses, style and system of play can allow the coach and players to set up realistic practice situations to give the team an edge when they eventually meet their opponents. By giving players accurate information about their performance from match counts and analysis, it is more likely that they will want to work seriously to rectify faults which will improve their performance.

The model of an evaluation system shown on page 141 explains how the process could be implemented at a club.

OBJECTIVE INFORMATION

The coach must decide what he wants to analyse and why. Is it an individual group or team? He may want information on aspects of his own team's play (e.g. re-starts) to check on their success, or to discover how often certain players shoot at goal, or to compare players in terms of their running loads. He may want to look at certain players in the opposing team, or at particular patterns of their play. He needs to be clear at the outset what he wishes to evaluate and what benefits will accrue from this assessment.

Methodology

Information can be gleaned from various sources – video film, training, practice matches, the live competitive match (which is often best), or feedback from his own players who have already played against the team. Modern computers and other sophisticated equipment are increasingly being used to analyse the performance of players and teams. Much will depend on the quality of the scouts and how well they can record details, as well as the time available to them. Valuable, objective information can be gathered without expensive equipment.

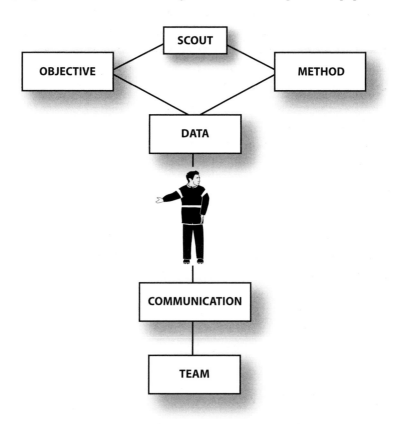

Data

The coach must sift the essential information from the scout's data so that he can pass it on to his team. It is vital that the scout knows exactly what he is looking for and the style of presentation required. It is best that a standard format is designed and used for this purpose.

Communication

The coach should look over the scouting report with his assistants to formulate the basic strategy and approach of the forthcoming match. The information should be relayed to the team, and comments from players who might know extra details need to be considered and adjustments made to the team preparation where appropriate. How and when this information is given to the team is important, as by building up the opposition too much creates doubts in the players' minds; passing on last minute tips also does not give players time to assimilate the new information and learn from it. Some coaches do not study the opposition because they feel it is more important for the team to deal with its own approach rather than think about the other team. This is more acceptable with a strong, mature and experienced team; however, in my opinion it is always better to scout the opposition so that there will be no surprises.

Scouting preparation

The coach may act as scout himself, or get his assistant or a scout to do the job. However, whoever is responsible should take the following steps:

- Obtain a fixture list of all the league/cup matches so that a scouting schedule can be organised in advance.
- Have a supply of standard scouting sheets prepared in advance.
- Get to the ground early to ensure a good, comfortable spot with a clear viewing position free from any distractions and where it is possible to concentrate for the duration of the match.
- Grounds are often badly designed for scouting purposes so make sure you dress against cold weather and have a clear view of the pitch. A high position in the grandstand is good for seeing tactical patterns and systems of play, while it may be better to be lower down and 'nearer the action' when observing individual players.

Scouting principles

A creative coach can design many methods by which the scout can analyse the performance of players and teams, but all methods should incorporate the following principles.

Simplicity

The scouting system should be simple in design and be relatively easy to administer and record. Complexity causes problems so whatever way you decide to collect and evaluate data remember simplicity is best.

Accuracy

The scout should ensure that it is as accurate as possible and keep to the objective without allowing other factors to get in the way. Try to make sure that you have set criteria that everyone understands as it relates to the match.

Efficiency

The scouting system should not involve the scout in the time-consuming chore of sorting out a mass of sheets, symbols or data. Instead it should concentrate on the areas that really matter and record them effectively.

Productivity

Remember that no matter how good the assessment looks or how much time has been spent on producing it, it must help the player or team to **improve their performance**.

The scout must try to be free from personal prejudices and record the facts as he sees them honestly and objectively. Coaches and players often disagree between themselves over match incidents. It is only human to try to prove yourself correct and to subconsciously forget aspects of an incident. The problem is often one of accuracy. The scout, however, will see incidents from higher positions than the players, who will be operating at ground level, while coaches will also see situations from different angles, distances and speeds. The scout must not rely on memory, but should try to collect factual information wherever possible.

Scouting material

Pages 147–159 at the end of this chapter contain samples of scouting sheets I have designed for professional clubs over the past two decades. Scouting can be applied in two general areas.

1. **Individual performance**

   This involves either looking at a player with the view of signing him for your club, or assessing one of your own players' performances during training or a competitive match to help him correct a weakness in his game. This can be of a physical, technical, tactical or psychological nature. See page 146 for a sample evaluation that I did on a player for Liverpool Football Club.

2. **Team performance**

This involves charting the opposition before meeting them in a match, or recording your own team's performance so that accurate information can be given to them at the match inquest. The form on pages 147–154 shows an actual evaluation by Everton Football Club.

Guidelines

The individual player or team being evaluated should, whenever possible, be assessed both at home and away to get a clearer idea of their total abilities. Different opponents, ground conditions, form and pressures upon players over a period of time will give a more realistic picture.

When relaying the results of match counts to players, care must be taken that all possible reasons for the final figures have been taken into account. For example, the count may show that the team's top strikers failed to get many shots at goal over the 90 minutes, when in fact their team was under constant pressure by a stronger team, they received scant service and as a consequence spent the majority of the match in defensive duties.

By keeping a regular assessment of his own team's performance over the season the coach can see if regular patterns are emerging. He may discover that the team has lost a high number of goals from left flank crosses, indicating a possible weakness. For the following season he may try to acquire new players who can defend better on this flank, or a more dominant central defender/ goalkeeper who can deal more effectively with crosses, or he may do intensive coaching work during the pre-season to improve this aspect of play.

The coach must sift the relevant data and present it to the team in a form that they can understand and apply. Care should be taken not to over-emphasise the strengths of other teams otherwise players can become anxious about their opponents. Conversely, complacency can creep in if the opposition team is made to look a pushover. It should be presented in an objective manner that conveys confidence to the players and indicates the belief that if the game plan is agreed to and carried out, then the team have a good chance of winning or performing towards their maximum.

Match counts

These can be based on individuals or teams and can be effective if used correctly and sensitively by the coach. He must understand the major advantages and disadvantages of assessing his own players' or team's performances. See the advantages and disadvantages table on page 156.

Summary

To be effective a coach needs some on-going objective evidence on which to base his team preparation and coaching programme. He has, of course, also to learn to rely on his experience – even the most accomplished coach needs to gather quality information about all aspects of his individual players, team and the opposition to ensure that he is heading in the right direction.

LIVERPOOL F.C. – PLAYER EVALUATION

Name: John Hendrie	**Age**: 27
	Height: 5'8"
	Physique: Strong frame
Team: Leeds United F.C. v West Bromwich Albion F.C.	**Date**: 24/02/90
Competition: 2nd division	

Venue: Elland Road

Score: 2–2

State of field/weather: Sparse, muddy field with continuous wind and rain

PHYSICAL
His strong build enables him to hold onto the ball under challenge on a heavy field. Got through a lot of work with many long runs with/without the ball and lasted the game well although just back after an injury. Quick, explosive from a standing start. His low centre of gravity allows him to change direction quickly where he can go past defenders.

TECHNICAL
Goes at defenders with the ball at his feet. Occasionally his 'touch' lets him down but overall he is a danger in wide positions. He can strike the ball well with both feet to cross and shoot on the run. Although he will challenge for the ball in the air, heading is not his strong point.

TACTICAL
Causes problems with his movement and direct play. At times he lacks a bit of creativity and goes down 'blind-alleys'. Not the best defender when the ball is lost, however he is always willing to recover and chase back to challenge for the ball.

CHARACTER
A gusty little player who never knows when to quit. He keeps going even when things are not always going his way and shows confidence in his ability. Loses concentration at times but overall he has a positive attitude to the game.

GENERAL IMPRESSION
He has pace, and considering it was his first game back from injury, he showed that it is worth following up on his continuing development. He does not always make the best of each situation, especially when in crossing, and some shooting positions. He is nevertheless, a dangerous player for defenders to deal with in wide or a more central position.

TEAM ANALYSIS – NEWCASTLE v PORTSMOUTH

Scout: Andy Smith

Report on: Newcastle United

Venue: St. James Park

Competition: Premiership

Date: 04/02/06

Results: 2–0

Scorers: N'Zogbia (44 min) Shearer (64 min)

TEAM SYSTEMS and PLAYERS NUMBERS

```
                    1
                  Given

   26        19        6        33
 Ramage   Bramble  Boumsong  Babayaro

   4         17        5        14
 Solano    Parker    Emre    N'Zogbia

            9         23
          Shearer   Ameobi
```

```
                   25
                Mwaruwari

   26            4           24
 O'Neil    D'Alessandro  Routledge

            30        28
          Mendes     Davis

   14        5        2         16
 Taylor   O'Brien   Primus    Griffin

             1
           Kiely
```

SUBSTITUTIONS

1	On: Dyer 8 Off: Solano 4 Min: 75 REASON: Tactical – straight swap
2	On: Bowyer 11 Off: Emre 5 Min: 75 REASON: Tactical – straight swap
3	On: Clark 21 Off: Parker 17 Min: 86 REASON: Tactical – No change to the formation

USED SUBS

3 Elliot
12 Harper (Gk)

CHANGES FROM PREVIOUS GAME

Solano on for Clark
Ameobi on for Chopra

SYSTEM/PATTERN OF PLAY

Newcastle played a much quicker passing game than normal, playing lots of one-touch passes with movement. Good width in attack was provided with N'Zogbia and Solano who looked to whip in crosses for Shearer and Ameobi. Parker broke everything up in midfield and worked well with Emre to play the front men in with through-passes.

PACE/LACK OF PACE IN TEAM

LIGHTENING	
SHARP	Solano, N'Zogbia and Babayaro
SUSTAINED	Boumsong, Parker, Bramble and Ameobi
AVERAGE	Emre (quick feet though), Shearer and Ramage
BELOW AVERAGE	
PEDESTRIAN	

HEIGHT/AERIAL ABILITY – POTENTIAL DANGER

PLAYER	COMMENTS
Shearer	Great technique allied to intelligent movement and uses his strength and timing to attack the ball
Boumsong	Impressive size and physical presence. Did not show much movement
Bramble	As above
Ameobi	Big awkward lad who showed good movement. Will attack the ball in the air and cause problems
Ramage	Often a target for near-post flick-ons at corner-kicks

TEAM UNITS

GOALKEEPER	
ELEMENTS	COMMENTS
KICKING	Will kick long from his hands if nothing on. Deals well with back-passes on his right foot but struggles on his left side.
THROWING	Looks to throw the ball quickly to his full backs if at all on – otherwise will kick long.
HANDLING	Had little to do, but was comfortable in his handling and dealt with shots and crosses with ease.
GENERAL	Given has a good all-round game and deals with most situations well although he occasionally loses concentration.

FULL-BACKS/WING-BACKS

Good width provided by both full backs who tried to get forward. Ramage did this more than Babayaro, and showed determination in delivering crosses, which were not always of the highest quality. Babayaro tended to look for the 'easy' ball although he has the most ability of the two. Both are good athletes who can get up and down the flanks.

CENTRE-BACKS

Boumsong and Bramble are very good athletes who always compete physically, however they will often give forwards a chance due to slack control or bad decision-making. With their size and strength they will win most balls in the air – they go forward at set-plays. They tend to leave the ball for each other at times and should be pressured at all times.

MIDFIELD

Newcastle looked very strong in midfield, especially in the central area. Parker was at the hub of everything they did, both in tackling and creating – he set the whole tempo of the game. Emre was quick, bright and tricky, always looking to create openings for others. N'Zogbia worked hard and was extremely dangerous when running at defenders with the ball. Solano produced some excellent crosses and wasted few balls although he is a 'light-weight' defensively.

FORWARDS

Shearer as always was the main target-man and did his entire running in the danger areas. Never shirks a challenge and never allows defenders to have an easy ride. Strong on either foot with great heading technique in the air. Ameobi is an extremely awkward customer and appears all arms and legs. Gets into good positions but often fails to capitalise due to poor decisions and a lack of awareness of situations around him. A willing worker who puts himself about.

RESTARTS

THROW-INS: Nothing special on either side of the field. No long throws. (*N.B.* When N'Zogbia takes throws, it often looks a foul throw.)

CORNER-KICKS: This was the basic set-up for their 5 corners, all from the left side.

1)

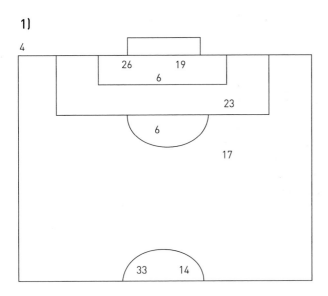

The first two corners were driven in right-footed by Solano 4 to Ramage 6 who tried to flick the ball on towards the other four attackers bunching in 6 yard box to crowd the goalkeeper.

2)

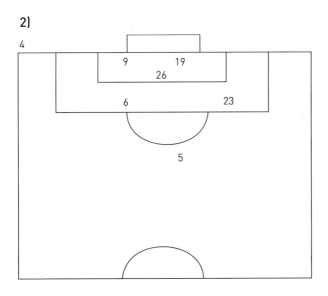

The 3rd and 4th corner was driven by Solano 4 further to the far post area for Ameobi running in to meet it

3)

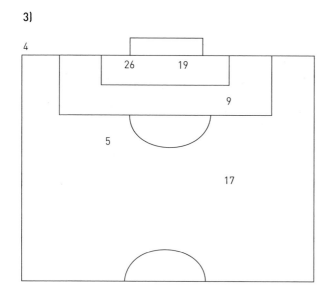

The last corner was played short to Emre 5 who passed it back to Solano 4 to cross full-time towards the far post where Shearer attacked it.

4)

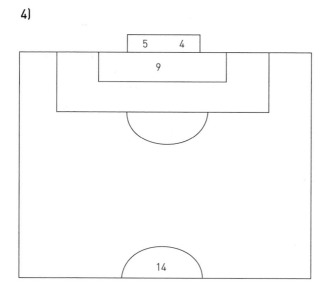

At defensive corners, Newcastle adopted this pattern. Emre 5 and Solano 4 stood on the posts whilst Shearer 9 was free to attack the ball. The rest of the players marked-up except for N'Zogbia who stayed up field.

FREE KICKS

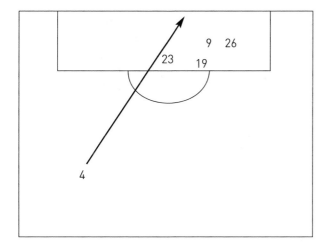

All four Newcastle players bunched together with little movement but plenty of pushing and shoving. A poor delivery by Solano 4 saw it come to nothing.

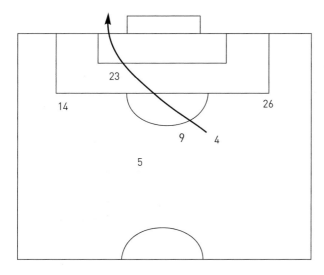

Alan Shearer 9 pretended to shoot and ran over the ball for Solano 4 to strike a right footed shot just wide of the post.

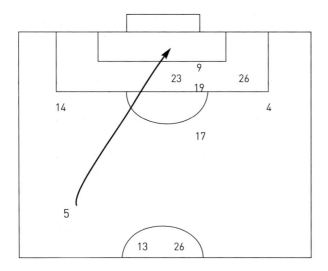

Emre 5 curled in the ball left-footed but put it too near the goalkeeper.

No.	NAME	COMMENTS
	INDIVIDUAL REPORT	
1	Shay Given	Quiet afternoon. Safe hands and out quickly when needed.
26	Peter Ramage	Willing runner, always making himself available for the ball up and down the flank.
19	Titus Bramble	Great physical ability and very strong in the air but prone to lapses of concentration.
6	Jean-Alain Boumsong	Good size, pace and mobile. Can get drawn out of position and leave gaps at the back.
33	Celestine Babayaro	Good athlete gets up and down the flank and shows glimpses of his ability. Not always convincing defensively.
4	Nolberto Solano	Nice close control and good crossing ability. Can go missing at times and does not go past people with the ball.
17	Scott Parker	Covered lots of ground, breaking up opponents play and linking up with team-mates. Effective all over the field.
5	Emre	Low centre of gravity allows him great control and very inventive range of passing. Does not do much work defensively.
14	Charles N'Zogbia	Very busy, can go past defenders on the inside and outside. Most effective when running at and taking opponents on.
9	Alan Shearer	Always a danger. Does not do a lot of running except when there is a chance of getting on the end of something.
23	Shola Ameobi	Good physical presence and an awkward customer. Quick feet but sometimes slower in thought, which affects his control.
8	Kieron Dyer	Replaced Solano on 75 minutes. Tried to add energy and enthusiasm but not 100 per cent fit as yet.
11	Lee Bowyer	Replaced Emre on 75 minutes. Put in a few hefty challenges but little else.

SCORING MATCH COUNT									
PERIOD		**FIRST HALF**			**TOTAL**	**SECOND HALF**			**TOTAL**	**GRAND**
Time/mins		15	30	45		60	75	90		**TOTAL**
SHOTS	✓									
	✘									
HEADERS	✓									
	✘									
CORNER KICKS	✓									
	✘									
FREE KICKS	✓									
	✘									
THROW-INS	✓									
	✘									

This simple match count is to collect data on the team's goal scoring attempts. Shots or headers which are a success (on target/score) are recorded with a tick whilst ones not taken or off-target are given a cross. The players' numbers are also shown and the totals can be analysed. These sorts of counts can be devised for technical skills, tactics or even players' behaviour during the match.

ADVANTAGES	DISADVANTAGES
1. Motivational It can aid motivation by showing improvement through comparison with others where the player/team performs better in some aspect of their play.	**1. Threatening** Sometimes players feel their play is constantly being scrutinised and is being used to show their weaknesses. They tend to feel threatened and treat the results gained from the count negatively.
2. Communication It provides the coach with a good opportunity to communicate effectively. The player can be shown clearly the areas where he should focus his attention and they can work together to progress.	**2. Credibility** The players can lose faith in the match count if it produces inaccurate information. If this happens, the coach will also lose credibility.
3. Reinforcement Evidence from match counts can be used by the coach to identify problems with a stubborn player who does not accept responsibility for them. It needs to be carefully handled, however, because the match count can alienate the player if used as a technique to threaten him.	**3. Time-consuming** It can take a long time to record, assess and analyse the data correctly, so it does depend on time availability as to how far your scouting can operate.

If used properly, information from scouts can help individual players and teams to perform more effectively. It is not foolproof, however, and should only be used as a guideline by the coach alongside his own knowledge, instincts and experience.

GUIDELINES FOR SCOUTING A TEAM

ATTACK	DEFENCE
BACK UNIT	
1. Which players are most comfortable on the ball?	1. Which centre back likes to man-mark?
2. Which players penetrate most with passes?	2. Which centre back prefers to cover space?
3. Which wing backs get forward to cross the ball?	3. Who are the dominant tacklers and headers of the ball?
4. Which centre-backs break forward into midfield?	4. Who has pace turns quickly and who does not?
MIDFIELD UNIT	
1. Who is the main 'playmaker' with the ball?	1. Who is the 'anchor man' who holds the central position?
2. Who 'breaks' forward for strikes at goal?	2. Who are main ball winners?
3. Which players play wide and can dribble and cross the cross ball?	3. Who hustles well, covers back or dives into the tackle?
	4. Who has a high work-rate and who hasn't?
FRONT UNIT	
1. Who is the main target man for the team to be played to?	1. Which strikers hustle defenders?
2. Who has pace, and attacks the space behind defenders?	2. Which strikers cover back and mark at set plays?
3. Who is good with the head and feet and posses main goal-scoring threat?	3. Which strikers are poor defenders at set plays?
4. Any good combinations between front players?	
GENERAL	
1. Basic system of play	
2. The tactical pattern of play (defence/attack)	
3. Characteristics of the team captain/players	

GUIDELINES FOR SET PLAYS

ATTACK	DEFENCE
CORNERS, FREE-KICKS, THROW-INS, KICK-OFFS AND PENALTY KICKS	
1. Name of player taking kick/throw. Type of service and accuracy.	1 Position of defenders. Man-markers or zone-markers.
2. Position of other attackers. The various moves employed.	2. Set-up of 'walls', etc. – clearing out fast for off-sides or not?
3. Players with special skills who present a threat to defence (e.g. strong shot, long throw or good header of the ball).	3. Dominant headers of ball.

GUIDELINES FOR GOALKEEPER

Set plays (as above)

1. Positioning for set plays – ability to deal with shots and crosses.

2. Who sets up walls and directs defenders?

ATTACK	DEFENCE
CORNERS, FREE-KICKS, THROW-INS, KICK-OFFS AND PENALTY KICKS	
1. Kicking – which foot, range, accuracy and direction.	1. General position for shots and crosses to support back unit.
2. Throws – accuracy and range, risk taking.	2. Ability to deal with shots, crosses and diving at feet in one-on-one situations.
General Ability to deal with pass backs.	3. General physique, height, speed, agility, strength and power.
	4. Mental characteristics of confidence, courage and concentration.

CHAPTER 9
PUTTING IT ALL TOGETHER

To be successful, the modern coach needs to be multi-skilled and bring all the winning ingredients together at the right time. It is widely accepted today that one person cannot deal efficiently with all the duties required to coach, and run or organise a good-class club. The modern coach builds a 'team-within-a-team' of talented, trusted people who can work together to get the job done. To get the most from this, here are a few guidelines to consider.

COACH ASSISTANTS

Often coaches select people they have known for some time and with whom they have a good relationship. They must agree on their general philosophy to the game and have a belief in what they are doing. Differences of opinion between the coach and his assistants are natural at times. After all, they are all highly motivated and work together in a stressful environment. They can differ over their tactical approach, team selection or disciplinary methods. However, it is important that the assistants have a 'voice' but having given their opinion, support the coach fully in whatever he decides. Remember the buck stops with him! Confusion can be avoided by forming a working procedure and simple rules and then sticking to them.

The coach should not always opt for assistants like himself. Often a combination of a few, but complementary, personalities are effective when dealing with players – the 'good-guy, bad-guy' syndrome, where one coach has a firm approach with the players after a poor match performance to be followed later by another coach who has more of a calm effect; between the two, they provide a sound balanced approach.

It is vital that there is mutual respect, honesty and trust between the coach and his assistants – success on the field can only be achieved by good teamwork off it.

ROLE OF THE COACH

The main aim of the coach is to produce the most successful team in the shortest time, and then build and maintain its consistency. The roles of the coach are many and varied, depending on the type of club and its aspirations and organisation. At some clubs he may just be responsible for the team whilst at others he may be expected to take a much more hands-on approach to the day-to-day running of the club. He must learn the skills of delegation, planning and organisation. He must not, however, be a blackboard theorist – he should be a practical person who gives thought to what needs doing and then acts on the best way to solve problems. The coach is the data-bank who stores knowledge, experience and resources which can be utilised for the team's benefit.

PLAYER COACH

Some people have been successful in this dual role, others have not. It is not always a guarantee for success that you have been a top player – some can inspire other players on the field by their presence, whilst other ageing players have begun to struggle with their own playing performance and have neither the playing ability nor the personality to provide inspiration. Some coach on the field, but lack the general coaching know-how to organise things properly off the field. Ideally, they should be able to do both jobs well but this is, almost always, asking a lot.

In reality it is a difficult task. It is vital that the player coach hires an experienced older coach who can take some of the load and allow him to develop through time. The player coach must not try to do too much – he must share responsibility. This will be most important when he is actually playing in match.

Does he give full responsibility to his assistant to make the decision to substitute him or others during the game, for example? All this has to be discussed and agreed between them if the role is going to work.

THE HEALTH OF THE COACH

The modern game, with its stresses and strains, puts coaches under increasing pressure which can not only limit their performance, but can also seriously damage their health. The coach must ensure that he maintains his health and fitness because the job requires continuous energy. The pressures are both physical and mental, for he will become emotionally involved with the team as its fortunes fluctuate throughout the season. The problem is that the coach does not have the same opportunities as the players to release the tension that they feel, leaving them more prone to mental stress. They have to balance their worries and problems, and maintain a balanced state of mind, which is not always easy.

They should find an outlet for stress, which could be a hobby, personal fitness and diet programmes, calming music or spending time with their family. It is important that the coach looks after his physical fitness, however difficult it may be. If the coach is very unfit it will be noted by the players and may affect their respect for him. He should take steps to correct the situation – maybe by asking another member of staff to design a health programme that the coach will adhere to.

It should be understood that coaches spend long hours outside in cold, wet and windy conditions. They also receive continuous criticism from an increasingly hostile media, supporters and their Board of Directors. On top of this, they have to contend with a squad of players which don't always see eye-to-eye with him – no wonder he needs a strong constitution!

Finally, it must be remembered that the coach and his assistant coaches and staff are the team behind the team, and are vital for the team's ultimate success. He needs to select his people carefully and set out to form harmonious relationships with each so that they learn to respect their abilities and character, and grow together. The most important factor is the coach and how he puts it all together to coach the professional way.

FURTHER READING

Allison, M. (1967) *Soccer For Thinkers*, Pelham

Cook, M. (2001) *101 Youth Soccer Drills (age 7 to 11)*, A & C Black

Cook, M. (2001) *101 Youth Soccer Drills (age 12 to 16)*, A & C Black

Cook, M & Shoulder, J. (2003) *Soccer Training*, A & C Black

Csanadi, A. (1972) *Soccer*, Corvina Press

Driver, M. & Nicol, S. (2003) *Coaching Dynamics*, Reedswain

Harrison, W. (2002) *Recognizing the Moment to Play*, Reedswain

Hodges, K. (2005) *Sport Motivation*, A & C Black

Tutko & Richards (1971) *Psychology of Coaching*, Allyn & Bacon

Wein, H. (2001) *Developing Youth Soccer Players*, Human Kinetics

Whitmore, J. (1992) *Coaching for Performance*, Nicholas Brealey

INDEX